Stars in the Same Firmament

OTHER BOOKS BY ANDREW D. MAYES

spiritualityadviser.com

Celebrating the Christian Centuries (1999)

Spirituality of Struggle: Pathways to Growth (2002)

Spirituality in Ministerial Formation (2009)

Holy Land? Challenging Questions from the Biblical Landscape (2011)

Beyond the Edge: Spiritual Transitions for Adventurous Souls (2013)

Another Christ: Re-envisioning Ministry (2014)

Learning the Language of the Soul (2016)

Journey to the Centre of the Soul (2017)

Sensing the Divine (2019)

Gateways to the Divine: Transformative Pathways of Prayer from the Holy City of Jerusalem (2020)

Diving for Pearls: Exploring the Depths of Prayer with Isaac the Syrian (2021)

Voices from the Mountains: Forgotten Wisdom for a Hurting World from the Biblical Peaks (2021)

Climate of the Soul: Ecological Spirituality for Anxious Times (2022)

Reforesting the Soul: Meditating with Trees (2022)

Treasure in the Wilderness: Desert Spirituality for Uncertain Times (2023)

Roads of Hurt and Hope: Transformative Journeys in the Holy Land (2024)

Another Christ: Rediscovering Jesus, Francis, and Discipleship Today (2024)

Transfiguring Life: Unleashing the Power of Paradox (2025)

Unlocking the Fountains: Inspiration & Challenge from Biblical Rivers & Springs (2025)

Stars in the Same Firmament

Discovering St. Francis' Interfaith Contemporaries

ANDREW D. MAYES

RESOURCE *Publications* • Eugene, Oregon

STARS IN THE SAME FIRMAMENT
Discovering St. Francis' Interfaith Contemporaries

Resource Publications
An Imprint of Wipf and Stock Publishers
199 W. 8th Ave., Suite 3
Eugene, OR 97401

www.wipfandstock.com

PAPERBACK ISBN: 979-8-3852-7300-3
HARDCOVER ISBN: 979-8-3852-7301-0
EBOOK ISBN: 979-8-3852-7302-7

VERSION NUMBER 02/11/26

PERMISSIONS

Unless otherwise acknowledged, Scripture quotations are from New Revised Standard Version Bible © 1989, 1995 National Council of the Churches of Christ USA.

The Message (MSG) © 1993, 2002, 2018 Eugene H. Peterson.

New International Version (NIV) © 1973, 1978, 1984, 2011 Biblica, Inc

The Voice Bible (VOICE) © 2012 Ecclesia Bible Society.

Extracts from Th. Emil Homerin, trans. *Umar Ibn al-Farid: Sufi Verse, Saintly Life* (New York: Paulist, 2001). Used with permission.

Extracts from Eva de Vitray-Meyerovitch, *Rumi and Sufism*, translated by Simone Fattal (Sausalito, CA: Post-Apollo, 1977, 1987). Used with permission.

Extracts from Charles Upton, trans., *Doorkeeper of the Heart: Versions of Rabi'a* (New York: Pir, 1988). Used with permission.

Extracts from Regis J. Armstrong et al, trans. *Francis of Assisi: The Saint- Early Documents* (New York: New City Press 1999). Used with permission.

Contents

"What a wonderful book! Seeing Francis in the context of other spiritual leaders and writers of his era has been a real joy, and resources us for interfaith interactions today. Opening a window into the insights and interplay of Christian, Jewish, and Muslim sages—men and women of Francis' time—it reveals spiritual treasures as precious now as 800 years ago."

—**David Walker**, Bishop of Manchester

"To sit down with our Christian, Jewish, and Muslim neighbors is Andrew's exciting invitation. There we will listen and learn to navigate by the three Abrahamic faiths' philosophers, theologians, mystics, and musicians who shine like stars in the sky—meet the contemporaries of St Francis of Assisi."

—**Pat Mossop**, Society of St Francis Third Order

"This fascinating book charts an intriguing possibility: What if St Francis of Assisi met and prayed with Jewish mystics and Sufi saints? Urged on by earlier female writers such as Rabia and Hildegard of Bingen, perhaps in Spain, or North Africa, could it be that Francis, Maimonides, and Rumi found themselves together lost in an ecstasy of praise and love for the unseen God? Mayes introduces their names, interprets unfamiliar terms, and stands back in wonder at the extraordinary religious fruitfulness of the thirteenth century."

—**Nicholas Alan Worssam**, Guardian,
Glasshampton Monastery, United Kingdom

"This inviting resource aims to stimulate and support Jewish, Christian, and Muslim interfaith conversation. Mayes' style is relaxed and informative—its easy flow of expression invites the reader to read more. This original, thoughtful perspective illuminates the tensions of St Francis' time in terms of the three Abrahamic faiths, and the character and faith of Francis himself. Hildegard of Bingen, Maimonides, and Rumi all feature in this carefully balanced work. Such tensions echo in our own times in contemporary antisemitism, Islamophobia, and nationalist identifying of Christianity for right-wing political ends. This innovative and practical resource for Abrahamic faith interfaith dialogue and group scriptural reasoning is timely, as we keep the 800th anniversary of a key peacemaker and reconciler, Francis of Assisi."

—**David Gifford**, Interfaith Advisor to the Bishop of Hereford

Images and Credits

Intro "The Trial by Fire of St. Francis before the Sultan" (c.1429) by Fra Angelico.

Wikimedia Commons. Public domain. https://commons.wikimedia.org/wiki/File:Giotto_-_Legend_of_St_Francis_-_-11-_-_St_Francis_before_the_Sultan_(Trial_by_Fire).jpg.

1 Hildegard receiving a vision (*Scivias,* 1151).

Miniature from the Rupertsberg Codex of Liber Scivias. Wikimedia Commons. Public domain. https://commons.wikimedia.org/wiki/File:Hildegard_von_Bingen.jpg.

2 Albert of Jerusalem.

Wikimedia Commons. Public domain. https://commons.wikimedia.org/wiki/File:Alberto_Avog.JPG.

3 Dominic meditating. Fra Angelico, San Marco, Florence.

Wikimedia Commons. Public domain. https://commons.wikimedia.org/wiki/File:Fra_Angelico_St._Dominic.jpg.

4 Jewish poet c.1250 conversing with cleric and women, from Codex Manesse (one of the most important surviving medieval German manuscripts).

Wikimedia Commons. Public domain. https://commons.wikimedia.org/wiki/File:Codex_Manesse_S%C3%BC%C3%9Fkind_von_Trimberg.jpg.

5 Fragments of Abraham Maimonides' Writing Discovered at the Cairo Genizah.

Wikimedia Commons. Public domain. https://commons.wikimedia.org/wiki/File:Cairo_Genizah_Fragment.jpg#file.

6 Nachmanides by Meir Kunstadt.

Image courtesy of William A. Rosenthall Judaica Collection, College of Charleston Libraries.

lcdl.library.cofc.edu/lcdl/catalog/lcdl:65034.

7 Ibn al-Arabi by Khalil Gibran.

Wikimedia Commons. Public domain. https://commons.wikimedia.org/wiki/File:Ibn_%CA%BFArabi,_Sayr_mulhimah_min_al-Sharq_wa-al-Gharb.png.

8 Umar al-Farid.

Wikimedia Commons. Public domain. https://commons.wikimedia.org/wiki/File:Ibn_al-Farid_by_Khalil_Gibran.png.

9 Rumi by Iranian artist Hossein Behzad (1957).

Wikimedia Commons. Public domain. https://commons.wikimedia.org/wiki/File:%D9%85%D9%88%D9%84%D8%A7%D9%86%D8%A7_%D8%A7%D8%AB%D8%B1_%D8%AD%D8%B3%DB%8C%D9%86_%D8%A8%D9%87%D8%B2%D8%A7%D8%AF_(cropped).jpg.

Preface

THE SPIRITUAL ENVIRONMENT AND firmament of the time of St Francis of Assisi was studded by outstanding luminaries whose voices are rarely heard in the West. This resource aims to inspire and stimulate conversations between the great traditions of Islam, Judaism and Christianity as we celebrate the 800th anniversary of Francis' life. We turn back to discover that the twelfth and thirteen centuries were a time of deep spiritual yearning across diverse cultures: stellar people making fresh discoveries of the Divine that speak powerfully to our souls today. As we learn of other spiritual pathways we rediscover afresh the uniqueness of Francis. Exploring the common ground shared between the religious traditions, we encounter distinctive insights that challenge our own ways of thinking about and experiencing God today.

Broadly, they moved in the same worlds, though we will not seek to identify a causality between them but rather celebrate the complementarity of these luminaries. We notice the constellations but will be cautious about drawing direct lines between the stars. However, we might be able to discern intriguing crosscurrents both of ideas and practice. We know something of Francis' own contacts with Islam in Spain and Egypt, while in his time, Jewish communities existed in many Italian cities, including Assisi, Perugia and Rome, giving opportunities for many informal encounters.

As we understand the spiritual aspirations and needs of the time, this resource will help a wide variety of individuals or groups navigate and explore the religious landscape of the 12th and 13th centuries. We will see how each star in the firmament draws us heavenwards, shining its transformative light into a world emerging from what used to be called "the dark ages"—illuminating contrasting perceptions of the Divine.

For students and followers of Francis this resource exploring the hinterland and wider world places his ministry in a broader perspective and helps us identify the uniqueness of his message as well as its commonalities and parallels with other contemporary spiritual seekers.

It is hoped that this can be used by small interfaith groups or study groups to provide an itinerary for shared reflections. This book aims to be a

- catalyst for interfaith sharing
- resource to open up wider contexts for understanding St Francis
- source book of Wisdom texts that will inspire lives of faith in the 21st century
- guide book to the spiritual life, highlighting perennial and universal themes
- text book for study groups
- material for quiet days or days of reflection

Each chapter gives an overview to our character, and provides a significant extract from their writings—if in a group setting, this should be read aloud, so that their voice addresses us today and speaks to our souls and minds. This book enables meeting Francis' Christian and interfaith contemporaries: encountering the Other, greeting and discerning their wisdom. How, then, should we approach ancient texts that come from a distant age or thought world? Philip Sheldrake writes: "What is needed is a receptive and at the same time critical dialogue with a spiritual text in order to allow the wisdom contained in it to challenge us and yet to accord our own horizons their proper place."[1] To this end, chapters include a set of penetrating questions to enable us to engage more deeply with the texts.

As an Anglican Franciscan (a member of the Third Order of the Society of St Francis) I am committed its principle: "The Order sets out, in the name of Christ, to break down barriers between people. . . Our chief object is to reflect that openness to all which was characteristic of Jesus." When living in Jerusalem as Course Director at St George's College, I wondered how I might somehow fulfil such a challenge. I realized that it must begin with listening and the avoidance of superficiality, so I set out to initiate conversations with people. This present book enables us to listen receptively to interfaith voices—from the time of St Francis—which will stimulate and

1. Sheldrake, *Spirituality and History*, 165.

equip us for closer attentiveness to neighbors of all traditions today. In Jerusalem, I was privileged to co-lead a small, intimate interfaith gathering at St George's Cathedral on behalf of the Anglican Diocese of Jerusalem, where two or three representatives from the Jewish, Islamic and Christian traditions met monthly to listen to one another's scriptures and to listen "with the heart." The group's practical guidelines for reading spiritual texts are reprinted here in the Appendix, in the hope that they will be useful for our own engagement with other traditions. Such readings have the potential to shift perceptions and open up new doors of understanding—the aim of this resource.

It is my hope that this book will enable an empowering and inspiring dialogue and interaction with Christians, Jews and Muslims of Francis' time, giving fresh impetus to our interfaith efforts and understanding in today's divided world.[2]

2. Our limit is Europe and north Africa. Space does not permit inclusion of such outstanding contemporaries as Soto Zen Buddhist Dogen or Jayadeva, composer of the Krishna epic poem *Gita Govinda.*

"The Trial by Fire of St. Francis before the Sultan" by Fra Angelico (1429)

Introduction

In the Scriptures of the world's great monotheistic religions holy lives are celebrated as shining lights or stars in the inky blackness of the night sky.

In the Hebrew scriptures the prophet Daniel declares:

> Men and women who have lived wisely and well will shine brilliantly, like the cloudless, star-strewn night skies. And those who put others on the right path to life will glow like stars forever. (Dan 12:3, *Message*)

In the New Testament Paul affirms his readers:

> You are the children of God, called to live without a single stain on your reputations among this perverted and crooked generation. Shine like stars across the land. (Phil 2:15, *Voice*)
>
> Shine like stars in the sky as you hold firmly to the word of life. (Phil 2:16, NIV)

Jesus says in the Gospels:

> Let your light shine before others, so that they may see your good works and give glory to your Father in heaven. (Matt 5:15)

In a revered *hadith* Mohammed says:

> My close companions are like stars, whichever one you have followed, you have been guided aright.[1]

Ibn al-Arabi declares:

1. Homerin, *Umar Ibn al-Farid*, 252, 253.

> The Friends of God are like stars in the sky: they shine with the light of God and guide those in darkness.[2]

The idea of holy people being called "stars" or "lights" from ancient symbolism in many religious and philosophical traditions carries both poetic and theological meanings:

Holy ones reflect divine light. In many traditions, God is described as pure, uncreated, eternal light. Holy people, through their purity and closeness to God, are dazzling and glowing examples of faith in practice.

Holy ones guide others. Stars have been used for navigation for millennia. Similarly, holy men and women are guides who help others find their way spiritually, becoming beacons in a dark world. (Mary is hailed by sea-farers as *Stella Maris*).

Holy ones dispel the darkness. Like stars visible against the darkness of the night sky, holy people in a world of moral confusion, injustice, and sin dispel fear and negative thinking. The lambent luster of their lives reminds people that goodness and truth are possible.

Holy ones radiate beauty and inspiration. Stars inspire awe and wonder because of their brilliance. Beautiful and uplifting holy lives stir us to higher living: glittering and shimmering in the world, they open up new possibilities of grace for us.

Holy ones mediate eternity. Stars seem eternal and enduring in the heavens. Holiness sparkles with a sense of immortality or union with the eternal Divine: calling holy people "stars" reflects an abiding effulgence, relevant to every age, incandescent and mysterious!

Holy men and women in every tradition who discover and share wisdom and truth can rightly be hailed as luminaries—having experienced some kind of enlightenment or illumination they become themselves luminous as they inspire us in the spiritual quest.

Guiding Light of St Francis of Assisi

St Francis of Assisi (1181–1226) was hailed by his first biographer, Thomas of Celano, in these glowing terms:

> At that time,
> through the presence of St Francis and his reputation,
> it surely seemed that a new light had been sent from heaven to earth,

2. al- Arabi, *Meccan Illuminations: al-Futuḥat al-Makkiyya*, II: 6, 49, 132.

driving away all the darkness
that had so nearly covered the whole region
that hardly anyone knew where to turn.
Deep forgetfulness of God
and lazy neglect of his commandments
overwhelmed almost everyone,
so that they could barely be roused from old, deep-seated evils.
He gleamed
like a shining star in the darkness of night
and like the morning spread over the darkness.[3]

In the next century Arnauld of Sarrant exulted:

Respondent as the dawn and morning star,
or even the rising sun,
setting the world on fire,
enlightening and making it fruitful,
the most perfect man Francis. . .
was like the sun warming that world
nearly covered by a winter of cold, darkness and sterility,
giving it light with the brilliant rays of word and deed,
dazzling it with truth,
inflaming it with charity,
renewing it with abundant fruit[4]

Many Stars

Bonaventure (1221–1274) reminds us in his *Evening Sermon 1262* that Francis is not the only star in the sky:

> We read that God said to Abraham: *Look toward heaven and number the stars, if you are able*. . .There is no star however small whose immensity would not fill the earth and give it light. Though the light and rays of each star coalesce in the atmosphere, they are found to be distinct when we look up at the stars themselves. It is something similar with devout souls whom the Holy Spirit enlightens with divine radiance. His posterity is as the stars of

3. Armstrong et al, *Early Documents,* I: 215. Thomas of Celano, "First Book".

4. Armstrong et al, *Early Documents*, III:678 Arnauld of Sarrant, "The Kinship of St Francis 1365".

> heaven, for the Holy Spirit brings forth devout souls in an altogether wondrous way.[5]

But there were other stars shining in the darkness of the twelfth and thirteen centuries. These stellar personalities were radical, pioneering, creative. Dominic even became the patron saint of astronomers! A legend circulated from his baptism, when his godmother saw a brilliant star shining on his forehead. This celestial symbol is believed to have signified his future role as a "light" to others. While he didn't study astronomy, this stellar motif was often depicted in his iconography, and makes a point!

TWELFTH AND THIRTEENTH CENTURIES: A TIME OF GREAT SPIRITUAL THIRST

The 12th and 13th centuries witnessed a deep need for spiritual renewal due to Church corruption, lay disillusionment, social upheaval, and a hunger for a more authentic, Christ-centered life.

The need for spiritual renewal in the 12th and 13th centuries arose from a complex mix of religious, social, and institutional tensions that were shaking the foundations of medieval life. This era, often seen as the birthplace or seedbed of Western religious reform movements, was marked by crises in Church authority and a growing lay hunger for genuine spirituality. Profound societal changes were weakening feudal bonds: Europe's agrarian population was shifting to urban centers, creating waves of change that affected all of life, including economic and social relations, politics and religion. The rise of towns and flourishing of trade fostered the growth of a new merchant class. Communities found themselves in transition: this was a liminal time, the harbinger of renaissance. This renewal was to take many forms: monastic reform, new mendicant orders, mystical theology, and grassroots lay movements, all of which shaped the medieval Church and laid the groundwork for future reform.

Challenges facing the Church

We gain an authoritative insight into the priorities and challenges of the Church of Francis' time from the decrees of the Lateran Council convened 1215. The largest ecumenical council so far, it consisted of more than four

5. Armstrong et al, *Early Documents*, II:729 Bonaventure, "Evening Sermon 1262".

hundred bishops and eight hundred abbots and priors of monastic orders. Its decrees reveal multiple failures that needed attention at the time of St Francis. The Council

- enforces the dogma of transubstantiation and elevates the role of priests.
- condemns the doctrines of Joachim of Flora/ Fiore, deemed an heretical Cistercian mystic (favored by the Franciscan Spirituals).
- establishes a procedure and penalties against heretics and their protectors, a precursor of the Inquisition (established in 1229).
- exhorts the Greeks to reunite with the Roman Church and accept its maxims so that there may be only one fold and only one shepherd.
- declares that the proclamation of the papal primacy was recognized by all antiquity.
- requires provincial councils to be held annually for the reform of morals, especially those of the clergy, whose excesses and corruption were well known. (The Council does not admit to the fact that many bishops and abbots lived in wealth and luxury, more like feudal lords than spiritual shepherds).
- identifies the irregularities of the clergy, such as sexual incontinence, drunkenness, avarice, hunting, attendance at farces and lewd entertainments. This was leading to a crisis of credibility and legitimacy among the clergy.
- confirms procedures in criminal law in regard to accusations against ecclesiastics.
- renews the ordinance of the council of 1179 on free schools for clerics in connection with every cathedral.
- forbids priests and deacons to perform surgical operations!
- forbids the blessing of water and hot iron for judicial tests or ordeals.
- requires every Christian who has reached the years of discretion to confess all his or her sins at least once a year to their own parish priest.
- directs that before prescribing for the sick, physicians shall be bound under pain of exclusion from the Church, to exhort their patients to call in a priest, and thus provide for their spiritual welfare.

- insists that Jews and Muslims wear a special dress to enable them to be distinguished from Christians. Christian princes must take measures to prevent blasphemies against Jesus Christ.
- makes rules for the projected crusade and publishes a range of indulgences.

Evidences of Spiritual Thirst: In the Christian Tradition

Meanwhile, the laity increasingly craved a more personal, direct, and sincere relationship with God. There was a growing lay hunger and desire to imitate the life of Christ, especially in poverty, humility, and simplicity. The Church was not meeting people's spiritual needs, evidenced by the fact that the void was filled by the rise of new lay movements, some deemed heretical.

Groups like the Humiliati, Cathars and Waldensians emerged as dualistic anti-sacramental, anti-sacerdotal sects criticizing the Church and offering alternative spiritualities. An inquisitorial campaign against the Cathar heretics was in full swing (the Albigensian Crusade, 1209–29). The popularity of these sects revealed real dissatisfaction with the institutional Church, especially its wealth and lack of moral authority.

Positively, the void was also met by orthodox groups: Bernard of Clairvaux (1090–1153) and the first Cistercians sought to revive the tired Benedictine tradition, such as the Cluniacs, while Beguines and Beghards were lay women and men embracing semi-monastic lives of prayer and service outside of traditional structures. Mystics like Mechthild of Magdeburg (1207–1282) , whom we will meet shortly, and Hadewijch (c1250) pioneered prophetic and visionary poetry.

Indeed, this was also a time of intellectual and cultural awakening. The 12th century renaissance brought a surge of interest in reason, learning, and theology. New universities formed, sparking scholasticism—a more systematic, intellectual approach to theology. Thinkers like Peter Abelard (1080–1142) and later Thomas Aquinas (1225–1274), sought to reconcile faith with reason, reflecting a renewed search for truth.

The rise of the Franciscans and Dominicans, with their radical call back to the basics of the faith, was a response to these times of spiritual yearning. We will meet Dominic (1170–221) who began his friendship with Francis in 1216 in Rome.

We'll celebrate Hildegard of Bingen (1098–1179) and early Rhineland Mystics delighting in music, the greening of the soul—with extraordinary correspondences and parallels with Francis. We'll learn too about Albert of Jerusalem (1149–1214) who lived in Acre, which Francis visited in 1219–20 soon after his death. It is likely that he heard about his influence on the first Carmelites.

Islamic Revival

The 12th and 13th centuries saw a religious, intellectual, and political revival in Islam. Saladin (d. 1193) recaptured Jerusalem (1187) and founded the Ayyubid dynasty which was to expand its influence across the Middle East. Thinkers like al-Ghazali (1058–1111) helped blend reason and spirituality, strengthening Sunni orthodoxy against both rationalist philosophers and heterodox sects, while philosophers like Ibn Rushd (Averroes, 1126–1198) defended rationalism and Aristotelian philosophy. The Islamic centers of Baghdad, Damascus, Cairo, and Córdoba blossomed as they witnessed advances in medicine, astronomy, mathematics, and logic, together with a flourishing of literature, architecture, and arts. As we shall see, mystical Islam thrived as Sufism became deeply integrated with mainstream practice.

We will meet Ibn al-Arabi (1165–1240), the Andalusian Arab Sunni scholar, Sufi mystic, poet, and philosopher who was extremely influential in the world of Islam and well beyond.

Ibn al-Farid (1181–1234) awaits us: arguably the most celebrated Sufi poet in the pre-modern Islamic world, with his poetry admired across both Arabic and Persian speaking regions of Islam.

Widely-translated Rumi (1207–1273) will surprise us with his stunning poems, and we honor his precursor and forerunner Rabia of Basra (c.717–801), one of the earliest Sufi mystics and influential female religious figure from Iraq and Jerusalem.

Jewish Renewal

The 12th and 13th centuries also witnessed a period of Jewish revival, though it looked quite different from the Christian and Islamic ones. It was a time of renewal in philosophy, mysticism, scholarship, and community life for Jews, despite living often as minorities under both Christian and Muslim rule. In the face of persecution in Christian Europe and political upheavals, Jewish life not only survived but produced some of its most enduring intellectual and spiritual traditions.

Moses Maimonides (1135–1204) laid the foundations for a philosophical and intellectual revival. He became a towering figure in Jewish thought, bridging faith and reason with his seminal work *Guide for the Perplexed.* While he was based in Cairo, other philosophers in Spain, Provence, and the Middle East continued his rationalist tradition. We'll learn from his son Abraham Maimonides (1186–1237), and Nachmanides (1194–1270).

And so we encounter the emergence of Kabbalah. These expressions of Jewish mysticism began in Provence and Spain in the twelfth and thirteenth centuries as Toledo, Barcelona and Girona became important centers, and bubbled up in parts of Germany. In the 12th century, Ashkenazi Jewry was emerging as a distinct cultural and religious group in the Rhineland and Northern France, having migrated to Central Europe from Italy and other regions. They were a part of a larger Jewish diaspora in Europe, primarily settling in the Holy Roman Empire, and were experiencing a period of growth and cultural development, laying the foundation for their unique traditions. We shall meet a constellation and cluster of stars in the persons of Judah of Regensburg (1150–217), Eleazar of Worms (1176–1238) and his wife Dulcea (c1115–1196).

CROSSING BOUNDARIES—OPPORTUNITIES FOR INTERFAITH INTERACTIONS

The travels of Francis opened up many opportunities for encountering other faiths.

Francis in Spain

Spain in the twelfth and thirteenth centuries was a region in transition. Since the eighth century, Andalusia had been under Muslim control (the Moors) which generally enabled a flourishing, side by side, of Muslim, Christian and Jewish traditions. Despite occasional polemic between them, Christians, for example, learned to appreciate Arabic texts: we know that Christians in Spain involved themselves in the important work of translating the Qur'an and other Islamic religious texts in the 12th century for Peter the Venerable, the abbot of the Benedictine abbey of Cluny (1092–1156).

Paradoxically, this was both a time of creative cultural exchange across the traditions and also centuries of struggle as, in the process known as the *Reconquista*, Christians sought to regain lost territory on the Iberian peninsula. Periods of tolerance and exchange alternated with conflict and persecution, depending on rulers and politics. The so-called Golden Age of Muslim Spain had been a period of significant cultural, scientific, and economic prosperity under Muslim rule, roughly from the 8th to the 11th centuries. During this era, Cordoba flourished as a global center of learning and innovation, fostering a rich environment where Muslims, Christians, and Jews collaborated on advancements in medicine, mathematics, and philosophy. Indeed, in the 11th and 12th centuries many scientific works were translated from Arabic to Latin: Southern calls this

> a considerable revolution, made possible by the changing relations between Latin Europe and its neighbors during this period. Despite the Crusades—partly even as a result of the Crusades—Christian and Moslem scholars met on common ground in scientific enquiry . . . permitting a measure of collaboration that had been quite unknown. . .The case was similar with regard to the Jews, who played a notable part in the work of translation and interpretation: the twelfth century witnessed. . .many acts of individual cooperation for scientific ends.[6]

Following a Muslim resurgence under the new rulers of North Africa, the Almohad Caliphate in the 12th century, their greatest strongholds succumbed to Christian forces in the 13th century after the decisive Battle of Las Navas de Tolosa (1212). To defeat their enemy, the kings of Castile, Aragon, Leon, and Navarre had created a union, a new turning point in the *Reconquista*. In 1212 these united forces of the Christian Spanish kingdoms, joined by Crusaders from other European countries, vanquished the Almohads in a reverse from which they could not recover. Now the Reconquest was progressing fast.

It was in the wake of this Christian victory that Francis made his first visit to Spain. Custato surmises: "Francis may well have been driven by an attempt (before or after the battle of 1212) to forestall any further bloodshed between Christian and Muslim forces."[7] Webster concurs: in the wake of the Christian advance, the climate seemed more favorable to the

6. Southern, *Making of the Middle Ages*, 66.

7. Custato, *Francis of Assisi*, 70.

Christians for their evangelistic work.[8] The rule of James I the Conqueror as King of Aragon, Count of Barcelona, and Lord of Montpellier from 1213 encouraged Francis to speak openly about the Christian gospel.

His visit to Spain probably took place in the winter of 1214–1215. The context of this journey appears to have been Francis' desire to proselytize in Morocco. Moorman tells us: "Having abandoned the proposed visit to Morocco, Francis spent several months in Spain, making new disciples and forming small communities in such places as Burgos, Barcelona and elsewhere. At Burgos and Ciudad Rodrigo the friars were housed in disused hermitages."[9] We do not know the exact route he took. Some scholars believe that Francis was offered a cell at St Nicholas' hospice in Barcelona, at the shortest sea distance from Italy. A late tradition even places Francis on the pilgrimage road to Santiago:

> In the first beginning of the Order, when there was as yet but few brothers and no convents established, St Francis went, out of devotion, to San Giacomo di Galicia, taking with him Brother Bernard and one or two other brothers. . . On arriving there, they spent the night in prayer in the Church of St James, and God revealed to St Francis how he would found many convents all over the world, and how his Order would increase and multiply into a great multitude of brethren. After this revelation St Francis began to found convents in that country. . .[10]

From an interfaith perspective, it is likely that Francis had opportunities to engage with Islamic teachers—as we shall see, Ibn al-Arabi and Ibn al-Farid were very popular and influential at this time.

Francis had travelled with Bernard of Quintavalle, his first follower, and John Parenti. Francis consolidated the early Franciscan witness in Iberia by first appointing Bernard as Minister Provincial in Spain. Then, at the general Chapter in 1219, Francis chose John Parenti as Provincial of Spain. After that the Order of Friars Minor spread so rapidly, and its labors were so successful in that country that, upon receiving the information, Francis broke out in loud praises of God.[11] Upon Francis' death in 1226, John was unanimously elected general of the whole Franciscan order, giving him a

8. Webster, *Els Menorets*, 23.

9. Moorman, *Franciscan Order*, 28.

10. Heywood, *Little Flowers*, ch. 4.

11. García-Serrano, *Friars' Influence in Medieval Spain*, 55.

wider context in which to share what he learned in his interfaith encounters in Spain.

A little later, the great Jewish mystic work the *Zohar* (lit. radiance, splendor), the foundational work and reference point of Kabbalistic literature, makes its appearance in 13th century Spain at the time of Moses de Leon (born 1240 in Castile, Dominic's birthplace).[12] The Zohar assumes four kinds of Biblical exegesis and interpretation: literal meaning, allusion, anagogical/allegorical, and mystic. The great scholar of Jewish mysticism Gershom Scholem observes:

> This fourfold aspect of the Torah bears a marked similarity to the conceptions of certain Christian authors of the Middle Ages. . .Did the Kabbalists derive this conception from the Christians? . . .The simultaneous appearance of the idea in Kabbalistic authors, all living in Christian Spain and all working with the same theory of the four levels, suggests that they had somewhere come across this idea of four meanings and adopted it. One must conclude that they were influenced by Christian hermeneutics. The *Zohar's* account of the four levels shows a striking resemblance to the Christian conception.[13]

Franciscans in Germany

Francis himself did not visit Germany, but at the 1217 General Chapter of Pentecost in Assisi, Francis sent out brothers on missions across Europe, assigning a group of friars to "Germania", which at that time referred broadly to the Holy Roman Empire. Their leader was Brother Giovanni of Penna. Other companions included Brother Caesarius of Speyer, who in 1221 became the first Minister Provincial of Germany. Founding early friaries in Worms, Speyer, Mainz, and Cologne, he entered into close proximity with the Jewish proto-Hasidics developing Kabbalah, whom we will shortly meet.[14] The Christian Rhineland mystics, as we noted, were not faraway: Mainz, for example, is less than 20 miles from Hildegard's Bingen. Both

12. One tradition claims that renowned Kabbalist Nachmanides whom we will shortly meet, sent the *Zohar* from Israel by ship to his son in Catalonia, but the ship was diverted and the texts ended up in the hands of Moses de Leon. (*Shem HaGedolim*, Chida *Sefarim*, *Zayin*, 8).

13. Scholem, *On the Kabbalah*, 61.

14. An early Franciscan friary was founded in Regensburg in 1226.

Jewish and Christian mystics lived in the same Rhineland cities, vibrant urban centers with cathedral schools, monasteries, and Jewish communities, side-by-side.

Indeed, the Rhineland in the 12th and 13th centuries was one of the most fertile regions for both Jewish and Christian mysticism. Though their traditions were distinct, they developed in close geographical proximity and sometimes in parallel, shaped by similar cultural and intellectual currents. Hildegard of Bingen led the way as pioneering abbess, visionary, composer, and theologian. To the north west lived Mechthild of Magdeburg (1207–1282): Beguine then Cistercian, in her *Flowing Light of the Godhead*, she combines visionary language with deep affective mysticism. Franciscans arrived in Magdeburg in 1223—did they get to meet Mechthild?[15] Meanwhile, in the nearby Low Countries in the first half of the thirteenth century Hadewijch of Brabant thrived as a Beguine mystic, writing in the vernacular about ecstatic union with God, love as central to divine-human relationship. Later Meister Eckhart (1260–328) became influential in the Rhineland as a great Dominican preacher, emphasizing union with God through detachment and inner transformation.

We've already noted the Hasidic Ashkenaz ("German Pietists"), the Jewish movement centered amidst Christian communities in the Rhineland cities of Speyer, Worms, Mainz. Both groups lived through the aftermath of the First and Second Crusades, which brought massacres of Rhineland Jews (especially 1096) and heightened religious fervor among Christians. This apocalyptic atmosphere shaped both Jewish and Christian mystical and penitential traditions, questing after union with God in an uncertain and unpredictable world. So on the banks of the Rhine and in its hinterland Jewish and Christian communities lived side by side under tense and sometimes violent conditions, developing rich mystical traditions. While they did not directly influence one another in textual terms, their parallel development reflects a shared religious climate of crisis, reform, and yearning for deeper intimacy with the Divine encountered by the first Franciscan missionaries to Germany. Gershom Scholem observes:

> It is in fact undeniable that certain popular religious and social ideas common to the Catholic West after the Cluniac reforms filtered into the religious philosophy of some Jewish groups especially in Germany. Scholars believed in a connection between the Christian mysticism of the period [12/13 cents.] and the Hasidic

15. Moorman, *Franciscan Order*, 70.

> movement. . .Mysticism was in the air and its seeds fell on fertile soil among Jews and Christians as their spiritual paths unfolded amid the Mediterranean cultural exchanges of medieval Christianity and Islam.[16]

Francis in Egypt

Francis' ground-breaking exchange with the Sultan of Egypt took place in the midst of war. In 1219 Christian knights of the Fifth Crusade besieged the city of Damietta on the Nile delta, an important entry point for pilgrims travelling towards the Holy Land. The Crusaders' mission was to open up the routes of pilgrimage to Jerusalem's Church of the Resurrection, which were in Muslim hands. Their strategy was the way of violence: they aimed to slaughter as many followers of Islam as they could. When Francis arrived in Damietta, he tried to dissuade the Crusaders from their bloody action, but nobody listened. So, accompanied by one brother, Illuminato, Francis crossed the battle-lines.

First he left the relative safety of the crusader military camp. Francis had to step into no-man's land which separated the warring factions, and, in order to reach the enemy camp, had to traverse forbidding defensive ditches and heavily-armed enemy barriers. On reaching the city of Damietta, he fearlessly crossed three walls. His aim was to reach the Sultan of Egypt himself, Malek al-Kamil, nephew of Saladin the Great who had taken Jerusalem in 1187. He was turned back at every point, but was resolute and somehow got past the soldiers guarding the walls that kept the two camps apart.

He succeeded in having an extended dialogue with the Sultan, who received him with deep respect. Sultan Malek al-Kamil recognized him as a mystic because he was dressed in brown robes just like the revered Sufis of the time. For his part, Francis saw the Sultan as a brother, and in the process learned a great deal about the foreign world of Islam, glimpsing new perspectives on "the infidel religion" which had been viewed in the West through the eyes of prejudice and fear.

Francis was changed by this meeting, and it left an abiding mark on his own spirituality. The litany on the divine names, *The Praises of God* which he composed later, after receiving the stigmata at Mount La Verna,

16. Scholem, *Jewish Mysticism*, 83, 84.

looks like a meditation on the Islamic ninety nine Names of God: "You are holy, Lord, the only God . . . You are strong, you are great, you are the Most High, you are almighty. . . You are Good, all Good, supreme Good."

In addition, during his time in the Muslim camp, Francis had noted the effect of the call to prayer (*adhan*) on the Muslims: some had immediately broken off their work for prayers, others had been reminded that the window for prayers had begun. In his *Letter to the Rulers of the People*, written after his return to Italy, Francis requested them to see to it that a signal is given to the people "by a herald" to inform them it is time for prayers: the forerunner to the ringing of Angelus bells punctuating the day with prayer, first recorded in Franciscan usage within twenty years of the death of Francis.

In the event at Damietta, Francis emerges as an intrepid and audacious risk-taker, energized by the love of Christ, as he breaches the walls that divided two peoples. His encounter with the Sultan is sometimes considered to be the first example of genuine Christian-Islam dialogue. Certainly it has inspired many to realize how walls can be breached.[17]

What transpired in the 20 days between the Sultan and Francis? In Part 3 we will investigate strong influences on the Sultan's spirituality—which he shared with Francis—including the formative role of Ibn al-Farid and Arabi. Here we note in passing that we have the name of another key influence on the Sultan's understanding of Sufism: Fakhr ad-Din al-Farisi, a Persian Sufi who acted as a kind of spiritual director to the Sultan, according to Massignon.[18] His writings, indeed, may have suggested topics for discussion between the saint and the sultan.

Francis in Palestine

After the fall of Damietta in November 1219, Francis seems to have left Egypt by February 1220, sailing to Acre with John of Brienne, before boarding a galley bound for Venice.

Albert of Jerusalem (1149–1214) had just died, but bequeathed a lasting legacy which shapes the lives of Carmelites to this day. Francis will have

17. Calabria, "Ibn al-Farid: Francis' Sufi Contemporary", 53.

18. Doubted by Welle in "Arabic Sources for the Encounter between the Saint and the Sultan". French scholar Louis Massignon, Franciscan Tertiary and admirer of Charles de Foucauld, affirms Farisi followed the great Mansur al-Hallaj (858–922): Massignon, *Hallaj*.

learned about the first communities on Mount Carmel, which overlooked Acre to the south: maybe James of Vitry (c.1160–240), the Bishop of Acre from 1216 told him of the developments.

We don't forget that Acre, though a Crusader stronghold, was also host to a Muslim population, and a Jewish community later (1267) to be led by Nachmonides.

On his return to Italy, Francis wrote his *Earlier Rule* (1221). In the light of all his travels he reached a decisive conclusion.

OUR PRESENT OPPORTUNITY

In his *Earlier Rule (Regula non bullata)*, Francis described two ways friars could minister to Muslims: either by being subject to them and living in humility, avoiding disputes, or, if the opportunity arose and it was God's will, by openly proclaiming the Gospel and calling people to conversion. This earlier rule reflected a transformation in his understanding of mission after visiting the Sultan in Egypt, providing a novel approach to non-proselytizing dialogue and peaceful coexistence, where friars were encouraged to be subject to non-Christian authorities for God's sake:

> As for the brothers who go, they can live spiritually among the Saracens and nonbelievers in two ways. One way is not to engage in arguments or disputes but to be "subject to every human creature for God's sake" and to acknowledge that they are Christians. The other way is to announce the Word of God, when they see it pleases the Lord . . .[19]

This marks a significant shift from the prevailing crusading mindset of the time, which was often confrontational and focused on conversion through force. Francis' vision in this rule laid the groundwork for interreligious dialogue, promoting mutual respect and understanding between different faiths.

In such a spirit of humility and readiness to listen and to learn, in this book we approach the texts and words of our Jewish and Muslim brothers and sisters.

19. Armstrong el al, *Early Documents*, I:74.

FURTHER READING

Hoeberichts, Jan. *Francis and Islam*. Quincy, IL: Franciscan, 1997.

Menocal, Maria Rosa. *The Ornament of the World: How Muslims, Jews and Christians Created a Culture of Tolerance in Medieval Spain*. Boston: Little, Brown, and Company, 2002.

Moses, Paul. *The Saint and the Sultan: The Crusades, Islam, and Francis of Assisi's Mission of Peace*. New York: Doubleday, 2009.

Peters, F. E. *The Children of Abraham: Judaism, Christianity, Islam*. Princeton: Princeton University Press, 2006.

Toaff, Ariel. *The Jews in Medieval Assisi 1305–1487*. Florence: Casa Editrice Leo Olschki, 1979.

Warren, Kathleen. *Daring to Cross the Threshold: Francis of Assisi Encounters Sultan Malek Al-Kamil*. Oregon: Wipf and Stock, 2012.

PART 1

Christian Luminaries

Hildegard receiving a vision (*Scivias*)

1

Living Creatively

Hildegard of Bingen (1098–1179) and Mechtild of Magdeburg (1210–280)

HILDEGARD OF BINGEN

We begin with Hildegard for two reasons. First, hers is a rare female voice speaking to us in precious writings, art and music from a time dominated by male writers. Secondly, though Hildegard died just two years before Francis was born, they are surely kindred spirits, testifying to God's mystery and delighting in creation through song, poetry and prose, their lives characterized by a certain liberty of spirit, spontaneity, creativity—and even impulsiveness! Hildegard described her vocation: "I am a feather on the breath of God."[1] She flourished as a musician and artist, Francis as a troubadour and poet. Both were paradoxically loyal to the Church while subversive and prophetic, Hildegard writing letters of correction to bishops, popes, and even emperors, Francis questioning existing mindsets by his very lifestyle and commitment to simplicity of living. Both model the interplay between *gravitas* and playfulness, freedom and discipline. These incandescent, effervescent stars surely belong to the same constellation! Their irresistible and indomitable spirits shine brightly to this day.

1. Hildegard of Bingen, *Scivias*, II.1.

We also meet in this opening chapter another Christian woman of passion and faith, contemporary of Francis, Mechtild (1210–280), born when Francis was 21, in Magdeburg, a central German city on the Elbe River.[2]

Hildegard was born in 1098 in Bermersheim (forty miles from Frankfurt in the Rhineland), the tenth child of a noble family. According to custom, the tenth child was often dedicated to the Church as a kind of tithe. From an early age, Hildegard reported visions—"the reflection of the Living Light"—as she later described them. These visions were unusual but she initially spoke of them only to a few confidants. At about age 8, she was given into the care of Jutta von Sponheim, an anchoress at the Disibodenberg monastery. Hildegard essentially grew up in enclosure, receiving religious education and training in Latin literacy, music, and scripture.

In 1112, Hildegard, around age 14, formally entered monastic life at Disibodenberg hermitage alongside Jutta and other women. When Jutta died in 1136, Hildegard was elected leader of the women's community. She began to assert independence, advocating for her nuns to live a distinct, vibrant spiritual life rather than remain subordinate to the male monks.

In 1141, at age 42, Hildegard experienced a powerful vision commanding her to record what she saw and heard. Initially reluctant, she eventually began dictating her visions, producing her first major work: *Scivias* ("Know the Ways"), a vast theological vision of salvation history, illustrated with striking imagery.[3] Her reputation as a visionary spread quickly. Church authorities, including Bernard of Clairvaux (1090–1153), endorsed her, and Pope Eugenius III (1088–1153) read excerpts of *Scivias* at the Synod of Trier/Reims (1148) , giving her visions official approval.

Around 1150, Hildegard was beginning to feel constricted and held back from her life at Disibodenberg. At this time, she found inspiration in the birds in the natural world:

> Birds symbolize the power that helps people to speak reflectively and leads them to think out many things in advance before they take action. Just as birds are lifted up into the air by their feathers and can remain wherever they wish, the soul in the body is elevated by thought and spreads its wings everywhere.[4]

2. Space does not permit us to explore Hadewijch of Brabant, another Beguine, 13th-century poet and mystic writing passionately of the agony and ecstasy of her relationship with the Divine. See Hadewijch, *Complete Works.*

3. Hildegard, *Scivias.*

4. *Physica: Liber Simplicis Medicine* (*Book of Simple Medicine*) composed 1151–1158.

She was finding that her wings, as it were, seemed to be in danger of being clipped, and God was calling her to fly and soar. She felt impelled to reach her fullest potential to the glory of God. She identified with the psalmist

> We have escaped like a bird
> from the snare of the fowlers;
> the snare is broken,
> and we have escaped. (Ps 124:7)

Moving to Rupertsberg near Bingen, she founded a new convent, which soon became a flourishing spiritual and intellectual center. In the 1160s she founded a second convent at Eibingen across the Rhine, which also came under her leadership.

Her visionary theological works included *Liber Vitae Meritorum (Book of Life's Merits),* and culminated in her *Liber Divinorum Operum (Book of Divine Works),* a cosmic vision of God's creation and humanity's place within it. She bequeaths to us over 70 liturgical songs, and even scientific and medical works: *Physica* and *Causae et Curae*—compendia of natural history, medicine, and remedies, blending empirical observation with spiritual interpretation. In addition, we have her *Letters*: hundreds of surviving letters reveal her correspondence with popes, emperors, abbots, and laypeople. Through them she emerges as a moral authority, advising, admonishing, and consoling across social classes.

Hildegard of Bingen was an outstanding artist and painter. Her visionary works, which served as a form of visual theology, are recorded in her illuminated manuscripts like *Scivias.* These intricate miniatures reveal her spiritual insight, unique artistic techniques, and complex symbolic language. She employed unusual methods, such as using the painting material itself to create depth and perspective, rare in medieval art. The miniatures are known for their intricate and sometimes difficult-to-interpret symbolism, inviting deep engagement with their spiritual meaning: her visionary art continues to intrigue and inspire.[5]

Unusually for a woman in her time, Hildegard conducted public preaching tours across the Rhineland and beyond. She addressed clergy and laity, denouncing corruption and calling for reform. Her authority as a prophetess gave her a rare platform, though she remained within the framework of obedience to the Church. She was not without conflict: her

5. See selections in Fox, *Illuminations.*

correspondence reveals tensions with secular rulers (even Emperor Frederick Barbarossa) and with local clergy.

In 2012, Pope Benedict XVI declared her a saint and named her a Doctor of the Church—one of only four women to hold this title—recognizing her as a theologian and teacher of enduring importance. Today, Hildegard is remembered as a visionary, composer, writer, healer, and prophet, whose works embody the intellectual and spiritual ferment of the 12th-century renaissance.

Creation and Humanity

Hildegard saw the universe as a harmonious, living whole, infused with God's presence. Her visions (in works like *Scivias*) describe the cosmos as a radiant, interconnected system where the macrocosm (the universe) mirrors the microcosm (the human). Nature was a divine revelation: plants, stars, and elements reflected God's wisdom and creativity.

Her cosmology intersects with her theological anthropology: men and women, made in the image and likeness of God, are invited to become co-creators in God's garden of the Earth. Not only are we called to be like "flowering orchards" bringing forth rich fruit in harmony with the seasons and the cosmos, but also to be gardeners by sharing in the care of God's creation. Gardens and fields have always been integral parts of Benedictine monasteries, and we imagine Hildegard at work in them, collecting her medicinal herbs while at the same time contemplating the messages of creation.

Greening of Soul and Planet

Surrounded by damp green forests of the Rhineland, Hildegard was inspired to see God's "living power of light" in all creation and named it *viriditas* (Latin, "greenness"), a word meaning vitality, fecundity, lushness, verdure, or growth. Today we talk about the "greening of the planet" but nine hundred years ago Hildegard celebrated the presence of the Holy Spirit in the created order through the idea of greening: "the earthly expression of the celestial sunlight; greenness is the condition in which earthly beings experience a fulfillment which is both physical and divine; greenness is the blithe overcoming of the dualism between earthly and heavenly."[6] For Hildegard, the wetness or moisture of the planet, revealed in verdant growth, bespeaks the Holy Spirit who "poured out this green freshness of life into the hearts of men and women so that they may bear good fruit."[7]

> If. . . we give up the green vitality of [our] virtues and surrender to the drought of our indolence, so that we do not have the sap of life and the greening power of good deeds, then the power of our very soul will begin to fade and dry up.
> Our thinking affects our greening power. . . The soul is the green life-force of the flesh. . . When we humans work in accord with the strivings of our soul, all our deeds turn out well.[8]

For Hildegard, the wetness or moisture of the Holy Spirit is the quality that keeps the soul alive, juicy, and creative, allowing it to flourish and grow. We need to stay drenched by the divine Spirit, the energy pulsating in every element of the universe, the divine lifeforce that flows through everything,

She invites us to see the world differently, overcoming the dichotomy of heaven and earth by glimpsing the heavenly action in the freshness of the planet, which mirrors the human soul. We are being summoned away from a pragmatic and self-centered consumer mentality, so deeply entrenched in our culture and mind-set, towards seeing creation as not an entity to be manipulated or exploited but a divine presence to be honored.

Music as a Pathway to God

Hildegard was also a musician of note, bequeathing us over seventy compositions. For her, music was necessary for salvation, because it was the best representation of the state of humanity before the Fall. If a person wanted to know what it felt like to be alive before the Fall, Hildegard believed holy music could take you there, as she writes in her *Letter to the Prelates of Mainz*:

> Music stirs our hearts and engages our souls in ways we can't describe. When this happens, we are taken beyond our earthly banishment back to the divine melody Adam knew when he sang with the angels, when he was whole in God, before his exile. In fact,

6. Peter Dronke, quoted in Bowie & Davies, *Anthology*, 32.
7. Bowie & Davies, 32. See Craine, *Prophet of the Cosmic Christ.*
8. Fox, *Book of Divine Works*, 85 (Vision 4).

> before Adam refused God's fragrant flower of obedience, his voice was the best on earth, because he was made by God's green thumb, who is the Holy Spirit. And if Adam had never lost the harmony God first gave him, the mortal fragilities that we all possess today could never have survived hearing the booming resonance of that original voice.[9]

Hildegard's songs celebrated God's presence in creation:

> O Holy Power who forged the Way for us!
> You penetrate all in heaven and earth and even down below.
> You're everything in One.
> Through You, clouds billow and roll and winds fly!
> Seeds drip juice,
> springs bubble into brooks, and
> spring's refreshing greens flow—through You—over all the earth!
> You also lead my spirit into Fullness.
> Holy Power, blow wisdom in my soul and—with your wisdom—Joy![10]

For Hildegard, all creation formed a symphony, every element contributing to the universal orchestra of praise.

Conflict and Rejection

Throughout her life Hildegard experienced many struggles with the powers that be—whether ecclesial or political. Toward the end of her life she got into big trouble.

Hildegard as abbess allowed the burial of a young nobleman who had been excommunicated (likely because he died unreconciled with the Church) in her convent's cemetery. Local clergy objected, demanding that she exhume the body. Hildegard refused, claiming she had received a vision from God affirming that the man had been reconciled before death. In retaliation, church authorities placed her convent under an interdict prohibiting the singing of the Divine Office or celebration of the Eucharist. Of course, Hildegard was devastated.

Hildegard protested in her *Letter to the Prelates of Mainz*, defending the spiritual necessity of sacred song, arguing that music mirrors the harmonies of heaven:

9. Butcher, *St. Hildegard of Bingen*, 12–13.
10. *O ignis Spiritus paracliti* [O fire of the Spirit] in Butcher, *Incandescence*, 131.

> When God created Adam, he placed within him the sound of every harmony and of every heavenly symphony. . .Since the Son of God has restored humanity, it is fitting that we sing with our voice to God, just as we were created to do. . .To silence the praise of God in song is to silence the joy of the soul, which was given voice to glorify Him. . .Those who forbid the singing of God's praises cut themselves off from the company of angels, who ceaselessly sing before the Lord.[11]

The ban was eventually lifted shortly before her death in 1179. Her long life of 81 years could now reach its crescendo and finale. And when she dies, the convent chronicles record a marvel: two brilliant streams of light crossed in the sky above her cloister, forming a celestial cross that lingered long in the heavens.

HILDEGARD SPEAKS

In the first vision described in her *Book of Divine Works* she sees a Christ-like figure:

> And I saw within the mystery of God, in the midst of the southern breezes, a wondrously beautiful image. It had a human form, and its countenance was of such beauty and radiance that I could have more easily gazed at the sun than at that face. . . [He said:]
>
> *I, the highest and fiery power, have kindled every spark of life. . .*
> *I decide on all reality.*
> *With my lofty wings I fly above the globe:*
> *with wisdom I have rightly put the universe in order.*
> *I, the fiery life of divine essence*
> *am aflame beyond the beauty of the meadows,*
> *I gleam in the waters,*
> *I burn in the sun, moon, and stars.*
> *With every breeze as with invisible life that contains everything,*
> *I awaken everything to life.*
> *The air lives by turning [earth] green*
> *and being in bloom.*
> *The waters flow as if they were alive.*
> *The sun lives in its light. . .*
> *The stars too give a clear light with their beaming. . .*
> *I remain hidden in every kind of reality as a fiery power. . .*
> *I bear within myself the breath of the resounding Word,*

11. Fox, *Book of Divine Works*. "Letter to the Prelates of Mainz", 354.

through which the whole of creation is made.
I breath life into everything. . .

How could it be that God, who causes all divine actions to come to fruition through human beings, is not active?

God created men and women in the divine likeness. . .

From eternity it was in the mind of God to wish to create humanity, God's own handiwork.[12]

For the soul passes through the body just as sap passes through a tree. What does this mean? It is through the sap that a tree is green, produces flowers, and then fruit. And how does that fruit come to maturity? The sun warms it, the rain waters it, and it is perfected in the mildness of the air. What is the significance of this? The mercy of the grace of God will make a person as bright as the sun, the breath of the Holy Spirit will water the person just as the rain, and thus discretion will lead the person to the perfection of good fruits just like the mildness of the air does for the tree.

The soul is in the body just like sap is in a tree. And the powers of the soul are like the shape of the tree. How is this? Understanding is in the soul just like the greenness of the branches and of the leaves is in the tree. The will, however, is like the flowers on the tree. The soul is truly like the power of the tree bursting forth its fruit. Reason, however, is like the fruit—perfected in maturity. The senses are truly like the height and width of the tree. Accordingly, the body of a person is made solid and is sustained by the soul. Therefore, oh person, you who trust your understanding as good and you who wish to compare yourself to a sheep, understand what you are in your soul.[13]

MECHTILD OF MAGDEBURG

In the thirteenth century, when the forests of Saxony whispered with both piety and corruption, a woman stepped into fire. Her name was Mechtild of Magdeburg, and she was no ordinary mystic cloistered safely behind abbey walls. She lived like a flame in the open air—burning, exposing, consumed.

At twelve years old, she heard God's voice calling her to love him with a passion that would shatter the conventions of her time. She later joined

12. Fox, *Book of Divine Works*, 8 (Vision 1).

13. Hildegard, *Scivias*, (Vision 4).

the Beguines, a radical lay community of women who served the poor and sought God outside the sanctioned orders of the Church. There she began to see visions: rivers of light pouring from the wounds of Christ, the soul rising in ecstasy like a falcon into the sun, the terrible beauty of Divine Love searing through her with both tenderness and terror.

She wrote these visions down in her book, *The Flowing Light of the Godhead* begun around 1250, the first known mystical work in German written by a woman. But her words were no soft pieties. They were dangerous, volcanic, explosive.

She denounced priests who sold indulgences, monks who lusted after power, bishops who lived in gold while the poor starved. Clerics sneered at her as a deluded woman. Her criticism of church dignitaries and her claims to theological insight aroused so much opposition that some called for the burning of her writings. She was threatened, hunted, driven to flee Magdeburg. Yet she never silenced herself. She declared that God's love was not to be rationed by men; it was a torrent, flooding every soul who dared to open.

In her visions, the soul was a bride ravished by the Divine Bridegroom; yet it was also a warrior, armed with burning longing, who battled despair and sin. To read her words is to feel the clash of light and darkness, the trembling sweetness of surrender, the dread of being consumed.

At the end of her life, she took refuge among the Cistercian nuns at Helfta, the same community soon to nurture Gertrude the Great (1256–1302). There, her final visions poured forth like the last rush of a storm: images of a soul drawn into the Godhead, so close to the Infinite that language itself broke open. She died around 1290, her body frail, but her words live with terrifying beauty.

MECHTILD SPEAKS

Her mystical book *The Flowing Light of the Godhead* combines intense personal love for Christ with a cosmic view. He is both bridegroom and lover of the soul and also cosmic Lord: intimacy meets ultimacy. Mechtild expresses the paradoxes in Christology: Jesus among us is a pilgrim trudging across the world, a poor worker, but also omnipresent Lord.[14] In prayer she addresses Christ in tender terms:

14. Tobin, *Mechthild of Magdeburg*, 286, 284.

> You are the feelings of love in my desire.
> You are a sweet cooling for my breast.
> You are a passionate kiss for my mouth.
> You are a blissful joy of my discovery.[15]

She also shares with us her awesome, expansive vision:

> One day I saw with the eyes of my eternity
> in bliss and without effort, a stone.
> This stone was like a great mountain
> and was of assorted colors.
> It tasted sweet, like heavenly herbs.
> I asked the sweet stone: who are you?
> It replied: "I am Jesus."[16]

She delights in the imagery of the Sun:

> The sparkling sun of the living Godhead
> shines through the bright water of cheerful humanity. . .
> You shine into my soul
> like the sun against gold

And she hears God responding:

> When I shine, you shall glow.
> When I flow, you shall become wet.[17]

QUESTIONS FOR REFLECTION

1. Hildegard called herself "a feather on the breath of God." What metaphor comes to mind to describe your spiritual life? (Notice that Hildegard asks whether you want to compare yourself to a sheep or a tree!)
2. How do you find yourself responding to the idea that you are called to be a co-creator with God? What might that look like in practice?
3. How can you develop your creativity?
4. Have you ever been held back—for whatever reason—from exercising your gifts or achieving your potential? What did that feel like? How

15. Tobin, *Mechthild of Magdeburg*, 111.
16. Woodruff, *Meditations with Mechtild of Magdeburg*, 108.
17. Tobin, *Mechthild of Magdeburg*, 152, 76.

does Hildegard's experience (there are at least two examples above) cheer you?

5. What resonances, parallels or contrasts do you see between this chapter's characters and Francis of Assisi?

FURTHER READING

Dreyer, Elizabeth A. *Passionate Spirituality: Hildegard of Bingen and Hadewijch of Brabant.* New York: Paulist, 2005.

Fox, Matthew. (2012). *Hildegard of Bingen: A Saint for our Times: Unleashing her Power in the 21st Century.* Vancouver, Canada: Namaste, 2012.

Haight, Roger; Pach, Alfred and Kaminski, Amanda Avila. *From the Monastery to the City: Hildegard of Bingen and Francis of Assisi.* Fordham University Press, 2024.

Newman, Barbara, ed., *Voice of the Living Light: Hildegard of Bingen and Her World.* University of California Press, 1998.

Uhlein, Gabriele. *Meditations with Hildegard of Bingen.* Sante Fe: NM: Bear & Co., 1982.

St Albert

2

Living Compassionately

Albert of Jerusalem (1149–1214)

The man destined to be hailed as *Albert of Jerusalem* was born in the green valleys of Emilia, Italy, around 1149. His childhood unfolded in the turbulent twilight of the twelfth century, when Christendom was tearing itself apart as often as it fought its enemies. From the start, Albert showed a curious mixture: the steel of a diplomat and the gentleness of a shepherd.

As a young man, he entered the monastery at Mortara and was elected prior in 1180. Soon after becoming bishop of Bobbio in 1184, he was appointed bishop of Vercelli. There, Albert's life became a crucible. Italy's city-states were a cauldron of factional hatred: nobles against burghers, papal loyalists against imperialists. Where other bishops chose sides, Albert chose the risky path of peacemaker, serving the papacy as a mediator and diplomat between Pope Clement III and Holy Roman Emperor Frederick Barbarossa. As papal legate in 1199 he helped end the war between Parma and Piacenza: against all odds, peace held. A man of frail frame, modest bearing, had achieved what armies had not.

But the true fire of his destiny lay far from Italy. In 1205, Albert was appointed Latin Patriarch of Jerusalem, a post as perilous as it was exalted. The Kingdom of Jerusalem, carved out by crusader steel, was at once magnificent and fragile. When the Holy City was lost to Saladin in 1187, the patriarchate relocated to Acre, a crowded, feverish coastal city, alive with merchants, pilgrims, mercenaries, monks, and spies.

Albert embraced the burden of leadership. He counseled kings, mediated between the fierce crusader barons, and negotiated with Muslim rulers. He became a steadying hand on a realm that might have fractured entirely without him. His enemies—there were many—called him shrewd. His friends called him holy. Both were right.

Seeking Balance

Across the bay from the bustling harbor of Acre, Mount Carmel rises majestically on the Mediterranean coast. There on Carmel, a band of hermits had gathered, seeking God in solitude inspired by the person of Elijah. They were struck by his zeal, dedication and awareness of God's presence: "As the Lord of hosts lives, before whom I stand" (1 Kgs 18:15). In about AD 500, a monastery of Greek monks had been formed and a church built on Mount Carmel. Now, in the twelfth century Latin Christians came, seeking to pattern themselves on Elijah's example. An early Carmelite narrative relates:

> We declare, bearing testimony to the truth, that from the time when the prophets Elijah and Elisha dwelt devoutly on Mount Carmel, holy Fathers both of the Old and the New Testament, whom the contemplation of heavenly things drew to the solitude of the same mountain, have without doubt led praiseworthy lives there by the fountain of Elijah in holy penitence unceasingly and successfully maintained.[1]

The first monks interpreted Elijah's "double spirit" asked for by Elisha (2 Kgs 2:9) as representing the union of both the active and contemplative life, the "mixed life"—an integration of contemplative prayer and apostolic action, and when in 1210 Albert was asked to write for these brothers a Rule to guide their developing lifestyle, he endeavored to strike a fine balance between action and stillness. Though he was writing for the monks of Mount Carmel, his guidelines can give us too valuable clues for ordering our life aright.

Albert's aim was to provide for the brothers of Carmel an integrated life, a life in which all time could be sanctified. Albert writes that "common sense is the guide of the virtues" and he proposes a carefully disciplined lifestyle that maintains a healthy equilibrium between four pairs of opposite commitments. Brundell observes: "Although the Rule of St Albert

1. "Constitutions 1281" in Smelt, *Carmelites*, 40.

is clearly an attempt to be an alternative to the detailed structural models found at the time frequently in the way of life of the monks, yet it is above all else a document of spiritual guidance for those who wish to learn how to live a life 'meditating on the law of the Lord day and night.'"[2]

His lasting legacy was giving to the monks of Carmel their foundational document—later to inspire Teresa of Avila, John of the Cross and Theresa of Lisieux—and which still shapes the lives of Carmelites today. He was martyred by an assassin in a procession on the Feast of the Holy Cross in 1214.

Francis missed him by five years but perhaps learned about Albert from Jacques de Vitry, bishop of Acre from 1214, who met him at Damietta and welcomed him at Acre, noting: "We saw the arrival of the friar Francis, founder of the Order of Friars Minor. He was a simple and unlettered man, but most lovable and dear to God and to men." The first Franciscans settled at Acre in 1217 under Brother Elias, and as we noted, Francis made his visit there in 1219.

Challenges from the Rule of St Albert

First, Albert insists on a balance between solitude and community, between being alone and interacting with others. He requires: "each of you is to have a separate cell", a space for living and praying which each monk could call his own. The Desert Fathers had taught "Go, sit in your cell, and your cell will teach you everything."[3] The cell becomes a symbol of the need to safeguard a space in our lives where we can be by ourselves, uninterrupted, and available to God in expectant, waiting, prayer

Albert recognized the need to safeguard and protect from intrusion a place of privacy. There are times, he taught, that we must be entirely alone with God, as Elijah discovered, in order to listen attentively and without distraction to God. But there are also times when the community must come together, and he directs that the oratory or chapel must be "built as conveniently as possible among the cells." It represents the call to shared worship, the community at prayer. So too must the brothers eat in a common refectory, where they listen together to Scripture, and labor side-by-side at

2. Michael Brundell, "Themes in Carmelite Spiritual Direction" in Byrne, *Traditions of Spiritual Guidance*, 64.

3. Ward, *Sayings*, 139.

the communal tasks. The togetherness and aloneness must be held within a creative tension, the one sustaining the other.

Secondly, Albert proposes a balance between work and prayer, activity and rest for the brothers on Mount Carmel. He insists on the necessity of work for each of the brothers: "You must give yourselves to work of some kind, so that the devil may always find you busy; no idleness on your part must give him the chance to pierce the defenses of your souls." Albert says of the daily round of labor "this is the way of holiness and goodness; see that you follow it." But the day is to begin at the altar and be punctuated by periods of prayer. The *Rule* requires daily attendance at the Eucharist, and Carmelites see in the experience of Elijah nourished by bread from God on his pilgrimage to Sinai a sign of Communion sustaining us in daily life. In addition, there are seven times for common prayer each day—the canonical hours of the Daily Office, times for recollection using psalms of praise and petition. The whole day is to be marked by an alternating cycle of work and prayer.

Thirdly, Albert calls for a strict balance between silence and talking. Silence must be observed from Evening Prayer until morning. "At other times," he counsels, "although you need not keep silence so strictly, be careful not to indulge in a great deal of talk." Once again it is a question of proper perspective and Albert gives as his maxim: "make a balance, then, each of you." However, Albert is careful to make provision for the sharing of problems as they arise. The greatest day of worship should be a day too of honest reflection and exchange: "On Sundays, or other days if necessary, you should discuss matters of discipline and your spiritual welfare; and on this occasion the indiscretions and failings of the brothers, if any be found at fault, should be lovingly corrected." There is great wisdom in this direction to deal with problems as soon as they arise, not to procrastinate—avoiding the mistakes of Elijah.

Fourthly, Albert's Rule recommends a balance between sharing of resources and having what is needful: "None of the brothers must lay claim to anything as his own, but your property is to be held in common; and of such things as the Lord has given you each is to receive from the prior—that is from the man he appoints for the purpose—whatever befits his age and needs." In this prescription he delivers the brothers from possessiveness and unnecessary attachments and encourages them to live in a spirit of simplicity, accepting gratefully what is needed for well-being.

Living Compassionately

Though these words were written for the first Carmelites, they point us towards a way to live without stress today. The *Rule* is not intended for slavish imitation, but is composed in a way that takes account of individual circumstances—for example, brothers are to fast during certain periods "unless bodily sickness or feebleness, or some other good reason, demand a dispensation from the fast; for necessity overrides every law." Albert understands human nature and makes allowances for weaknesses. His rule of thumb is "See that the bounds of common sense are not exceeded." He is aware that this will be a struggle, and is emphatic: "you must use every care to clothe yourselves in God's armor so that you may be ready to withstand the enemy's ambush."

He offers his *Rule* in the spirit of a caring father. Like Benedict (480–547) before him, he writes his *Rule* with a compassionate heart: while he sees the need for discipline, he is well aware of human foibles and human needs. Benedict had set a wise example:

> Therefore we intend to establish a school for the Lord's service. In drawing up its regulations, we hope to set down nothing harsh, nothing burdensome. The good of all concerned, however, may prompt us to a little strictness in order to amend faults and to safeguard love. . . Brothers who are sick or weak should be given a type of work or craft that will keep them busy without overwhelming them or driving them away. The abbot must take their infirmities into account.[4]

Albert's *Rule* invites us to examine our lives and seek a sense of wholeness. Is there, for us, a balance between the needs of body, of mind, of spirit? If anything gets out of proportion—if there is work without prayer, or interaction with others without space for solitude—stress will result. It can be prevented, however, if we apply the principles Albert advocates for those first Carmelites, who tried to apply to themselves the lessons of Elijah's life.

The *Rule of St Albert* encouraged the spread of Carmelite communities throughout Europe. But over time, things began to get out of kilter. When Teresa of Avila entered Carmelite life in sixteenth century Spain, she was horrified to discover how far Albert's *Primitive* or *Original Rule* had been distorted and corrupted. There were too many material comforts and an acquisitiveness had crept into the religious houses. But most of all she was

4. Fry, *Rule of St Benedict*, Prologue and 48.

dismayed by the imbalance between prayer and ministry. The sisters were forever leaving the enclosure to engage in "good works" and pastoral visiting, but there was little time for solitude left. Things had got out of balance. Teresa felt called to reform the Carmelite order and to invite her brothers and sisters to return to the basic disciplines of prayer and contemplation. She wrote: "This, my sisters, I should like us to strive to attain: we should desire and engage in prayer, not for our enjoyment, but for the sake of acquiring this strength which fits us for service."[5] Teresa recognized that without prayer, all our labors can be empty of meaning and of power; by prayer we are energized by God and can become channels and instruments of his grace. Let us listen to his voice:

ALBERT SPEAKS

> Albert, called by God's favor to be Patriarch of the Church of Jerusalem, bids health in the Lord and the blessing of the Holy Spirit to his beloved sons in Christ, and the other hermits under obedience to him, who live near the spring on Mount Carmel.
>
> Many and varied are the ways in which our saintly forefathers laid down how everyone, whatever his station or the kind of life he has chosen, should live a life of allegiance to Jesus Christ—how, pure in heart and steadfast in conscience, he must be unswerving in the service of his Master.
>
> It is to me, however, that you have come for a rule of life in keeping with your avowed purpose, a rule you may hold fast to henceforward; and therefore:
>
> If the Prior and brothers see fit, you may have foundations in solitary places, or where you are given a site that is suitable and convenient for the observance proper to your Order.
>
> Next, each of you is to have a separate cell, situated as the land you propose to occupy may dictate, and allotted by disposition of the Prior with the agreement of the other brothers, or the more mature among them. . . . .
>
> However, you are to eat whatever may have been given you in a common refectory, listening together meanwhile to a reading from Holy Scripture where that can be done without difficulty.
>
> Each one of you is to stay in his own cell or nearby, pondering the Lord's law day and night and keeping watch at his prayer unless attending to some other duty.

5. Teresa of Avila, *Interior Castle,* 148.

Those who know their letters and how to read the psalms should, for each of the hours, say those our holy forefathers laid down, and according to the Church's approved custom. . .

None of the brothers must lay claim to anything as his own, but your property is to be held in common; and each is to receive from the Prior—that is from the brother he appoints for the purpose—whatever befits his age and needs. . .

An oratory should be built as conveniently as possible among the cells, where, if it can be done without difficulty, you are to gather each morning to hear Mass.

On Sundays too, or other days if necessary, you should discuss matters of discipline and your spiritual welfare; and on this occasion the indiscretions and failings of the brothers, if any be found at fault, should be lovingly corrected.

You are to fast every day, except Sundays, from the feast of the Exaltation of the Holy Cross until Easter Day, unless bodily sickness or feebleness, or some other good reason, demand a dispensation from the fast; for necessity overrides every law.

Since man's life on earth is a time of trial, and all who live devotedly in Christ must undergo persecution, and the devil your foe is on the prowl like a roaring lion looking for prey to devour, you must use every care to clothe yourselves in God's armor so that you may be ready to withstand the enemy's ambush. . .

You must give yourselves to work of some kind, so that the devil may always find you busy; no idleness on your part must give him a chance to pierce the defenses of your souls. . .This is the way of holiness and goodness: see that you follow it.

The Apostle would have us keep silence, for in silence he tells us to work. As the Prophet also makes known to us: "Silence is the way to foster holiness." Elsewhere he says: "Your strength will lie in silence and hope." For this reason I lay down that you are to keep silence from Vespers until Morning Prayer the next day. At other times, although you need not keep silence so strictly, be careful not to indulge in a great deal of talk, for, as Scripture has it—and experience teaches us no less—"sin will not be wanting where there is much talk, and he who is careless in speech will come to harm"; and elsewhere: "The use of many words brings harm to the speaker's soul." And our Lord says in the Gospel: "Every rash word uttered will have to be accounted for on judgement day."

Make a balance then, each of you, to weigh his words in; keep a tight rein on your mouths, lest you should stumble and fall in speech, and your fall be irreparable and prove mortal. Like the

> Prophet, watch your step lest your tongue give offense, and employ every care in keeping silent, which is the way to foster holiness. . .
>
> Here then are the few points I have written down to provide you with a standard of conduct to live up to; but our Lord, at his second coming will reward anyone who does more than he is obliged to do. See that the bounds of common sense are not exceeded, however, for common sense is the guide of the virtues.[6]

QUESTIONS FOR REFLECTION

1. In what ways does Albert exemplify the reconciliation of opposites? Consider both his life and his teaching.
2. Take another look at the four pairs of commitments considered by St Albert. What do they say to your lifestyle? Do you need to make any changes?
3. How do you balance the needs of body, of mind, of spirit?
4. In what ways is your life that of a mystic or that of a prophet? Can you be both at the same time—a "contemplative in action"?
5. In what ways does Albert's teaching in the Rule resonate with the experience of Francis as he sought to balance action and contemplation? What resonances, parallels or contrasts do you see between this chapter's character and Francis of Assisi?

FURTHER READING

Mullins, Patrick. *The Carmelites and St Albert of Jerusalem: Origins and Identity.* Rome: Edizioni Carmelitane, 2015.

McGreal, Wilfred. *At the Fountain of Elijah: The Carmelite Tradition.* London: Darton, Longman and Todd, 1999.

Welch, John. *The Carmelite Way: An Ancient Path for Today's Pilgrim.* Leominster: Gracewing, 1996.

6. Obbard, *Land of Carmel*, 39–44. "The Rule of St Albert" trans. Bede Edwards.

Dominic meditating, by Fra Angelico.

3

Living Prophetically

Dominic (1170—1221)

THE BOY WHO WOULD one day set the world aflame was born in a rugged corner of Castile in 1170. His name was Dominic de Guzman, but there was nothing of the courtier or nobleman in him.

He studied theology at Palencia. When famine struck Spain in 1191, Dominic did something that startled even his fellow students: he sold everything, even his precious manuscripts, the books he had painstakingly gathered, the very tools of his scholarship. "I will not study dead skins," he said, "while living people starve." The gesture was reckless, but it revealed the shape of his soul: mercy was worth more to him than knowledge.

At the age of 24, Dominic was ordained as a priest and joined the canonry of the cathedral of Osma in northern Spain. Dominic sensed an unfolding vocation when, in 1204, traveling with his bishop Diego through the hills of southern France, he came face to face with the crises of his age. Town after town lay in the grip of Catharism: villagers who had abandoned the Church for that bleak, demanding faith that despised the material world. Wealthy clergy arrived to argue them back, cloaked in silk and mounted on fine horses. The people listened, nodded politely, and turned away unmoved. Dominic saw immediately what was wrong: truth preached without witness was no truth at all. Wood explains

> Diego not only told the clergy [engaged in preaching against the Cathars] that the wealth and ostentation of their entourage

> undermined their message, but when pressed to provide leadership, he undertook to provide an example, sending away his horses, fine clothing, and retinue. Soon, Diego and Dominic were effectively leading the preaching mission to the Albigensians, for whom apostolic simplicity and poverty were essential emblems of holiness.[1]

So Dominic stripped himself of everything. No horse, no servants, no gold. Just worn sandals and a voice that carried with clarity and fire. He slept in fields, prayed in chapels, and walked endlessly from village to village, not only speaking but listening—listening to their doubts, their hunger for integrity, their disappointment in the institutional Church.

Dominic began to see the need for a new kind of brotherhood, a community of preachers bound by simplicity, study, and ceaseless mission. Not monks hidden away behind monastery walls, but men who would stride into cities and marketplaces and universities. From this dream was born the Order of Preachers, who would spread from Toulouse to Paris, Rome, and beyond. Dominic adopted the Rule of St Augustine for what was soon called the Dominican Order. Many houses of the emerging order were based near universities, which were beginning to burgeon at this time. Dominic saw the need for engagement, not only with the poor—his order was mendicant, that is, begging, dependent on alms not inheritances—but with the finest minds of his age. He and his order lived in poverty, which he saw as essential for effective itinerant preaching and for gaining the trust of ordinary people.

He displayed the rare combination of being capable of erudite theological exchange with professors and speaking the language of the poor. He was known for his profound prayer life, zeal for truth, and deep compassion for suffering souls. His dual commitment to poverty and intellectual study formed the basis of his order's mission to combat heresy through preaching and teaching.

Tradition holds that during Dominic's second visit to Rome, in 1216, he met Francis of Assisi in one of the churches there. Both were negotiating with the Holy See through their mutual patron, Cardinal Ugolino, later Pope Gregory IX, to obtain papal confirmation of their respective orders—the Order of Preachers and the Order of Friars Minor. Having seen Francis in a vision the night before, Dominic recognized him and rushed to greet him. A close friendship sprang up between the two, and to this day Dominicans

1. Woods, *Dominican Tradition*, 29.

and Franciscans exchange visits on each other's founder's feast days as a sign of unity towards a common goal. The mutual influences of Dominic and Francis can be seen in the development of their orders: Francis may have influenced Dominic to expand the practice of the vow of poverty, and the Friars Minor adopted the Dominican constitutional system as a result of their turbulent history after Francis' death.

One of his religious daughters, Cecilia Cesarini, among the first nuns to receive the Dominican habit, has left us a detailed word-portrait of her spiritual father: "Blessed Dominic was of medium height and of slight build. His countenance was beautiful, of fair complexion, with light auburn hair and beard and luminous eyes. A kind of radiance shone from his brow, inspiring love and reverence in all. Full of joy, he seemed ever ready to smile, unless moved to pity by the affliction of his neighbor. His hands were long and shapely; his voice strong, noble, and sonorous."[2] It is not surprising that a soul like Dominic's, at once gentle, strong, and ardent, radiated its inner strength through feeble and transparent clay without loss or diminution.

His nights were longer than his days. While his brothers slept, he would lie prostrate before the altar, whispering through tears, "Lord, what will become of sinners?" He seemed unable to accept the idea that a single soul might slip away from God's embrace.

By the summer of 1221, his body was failing. Years of fasting, walking, and sleepless nights had worn him thin. In Bologna, when his brothers begged him to rest on a bed, he refused. He lay on the bare earth instead, whispering that he belonged nowhere else. Around him, the community he had built wept, not ready to let him go. According to Dominican tradition, his final words were: "Do not weep. I will be more useful to you where I go than I have been here."[3]

Yet his story did not end. The fire he lit—of study, of preaching, of truth lived in simplicity—still burns across centuries, a reminder that one man's hunger for God can change the course of history.

Dominic's Prophetic Mission

In describing Dominic's mission as prophetic we need to ask ourselves: what *is* a prophet ?

2. Mandonnet, *St. Dominic and His Work.*
3. no extant primary source.

The burden of the Hebrew prophets was not prediction of the future, but rather declaring God's word into the present situation, naming the idols and illusions of contemporary society: forth-telling rather than foretelling, unpicking the meaning of events and circumstances rather than predicting. For example, Amos was concerned to deliver his people from self-satisfying rituals and self-absorbing forms of prayer and alert them to the desperate needs of the society around them:

> I hate, I despise your festivals . . .
> But let justice roll down like waters,
> And righteousness like an ever-flowing stream. (Amos 5: 21, 24)

In similar vein Isaiah is uncompromising:

> Is this not the fast that I choose: To loosen the bonds of injustice,
> To undo the thongs of the yoke, To let the oppressed go free . . .
> Is it not to share your bread with the hungry . . . ? (Isa 58:6,7)

Walter Brueggeman in his classic *The Prophetic Imagination* tells us that the role of the prophet is to envision an alternative consciousness, and to open up for people a different vision of things: Jesus himself was often hailed as a prophet[4], his message about the Kingdom of God directly questioning the prevailing status quo of the Kingdom of Rome. The role of the prophet is to enable an alternative perspective which may be subversive, questioning, compassionate, and which certainly reveals itself in counter-cultural lifestyle and political choices.

The mission of the Order of Preachers, the Dominican Order is to share with others the truth about the God whom we contemplate in our hearts. Their motto *Contemplare et contemplata aliis trader,* often attributed to Thomas Aquinas, translates as "to contemplate and to give to others the fruits of contemplation." Although the Dominican Order is officially named the Order of Preachers, from the earliest days, Dominic made it clear that without study, prayer, and meditation, the preacher has nothing to offer.

Veritas (Truth) is another key word in the Dominican vocabulary. Through scriptural, theological and secular study followers of Dominic readied themselves to confront error in the world and proclaim the one who said "I am the Truth!" (John 14:6). Dannhausen and Poochigian put it:

> Amid the chaos and insecurities of his time, with religious and civic life mired in corruption, Dominic's conviction was that

4. Matt 21:46; Mark 6:4; Luke 7:16, 13:33; John 4:19, 6:14, 7:40, 9:17.

> people needed to hear preaching that was authentic and true to the gospel. He believed that this preaching needed to offer people a genuine understanding of their real concerns as they struggled to adjust to the rapidly changing circumstances surrounding them. Above all, the preaching had to focus on the truth of God's mercy and love. This meant that it had to come from persons whose lives were firmly planted in the word they proclaimed.[5]

At first, Dominic found the heretics he encountered unreceptive, stubborn, and often hostile. But he gained the nickname the "Hound of the Lord" because he would not give up his barking! In preaching fueled by study and prayer, Dominic's humility, patience, and joyfulness under persecution impressed even his enemies, who at times mocked, spat at him, and pelted him with stones or mud. Dominic found the resources in his spirituality to withstand such onslaughts.

Embodied Spirituality

Dominic was concerned not only to unite mind and heart, study and prayer, he was also intent in uniting body and soul. We gain an insight into his embodied prayer practice in a document called *The Nine Ways of Prayer of St. Dominic* written by an anonymous author, probably at Bologna, between 1260 and 1288. Scholars believe that these ways of prayer were the actual practice of Dominic. In this experience of bodily prayer, the soul is lifted to God in praise, contrition, thanksgiving, and supplication. These ways of prayer are a glimpse into the inner life of Dominic and his intense love for God.

> *First Way of Prayer: Bowing.* First of all, bowing humbly before the altar as if Christ, whom the altar signifies, were really and personally present and not just symbolically. As it says, "The prayer of the person who humbles himself will pierce the clouds" (Ecclus 35:21). So the holy father, standing with his body erect, would bow his head and his heart humbly before Christ his Head, considering his own servile condition and the outstanding nobility of Christ, and giving himself up entirely to venerating him.
>
> *Second Way of Prayer: Prostration.* St. Dominic also often used to pray throwing himself down on the ground, flat on his face, and then his heart would be pricked with compunction and he would blush at himself and say, sometimes loudly enough for it

5. Dannhausen and Poochigian, "Dominic's Charism".

actually to be heard, the words from the gospel, "Lord, be merciful to me, a sinner" (Luke 18:13).

Third Way of Prayer: Penance. Rising up from the ground, he used to discipline himself with an iron chain saying, "Your discipline has set me straight towards my goal" (Ps 17:36).

Fourth Way of Prayer: Genuflection. After this, St. Dominic, standing before the altar or in the chapter room, would fix his gaze on the crucifix, looking intently at Christ on the cross and kneeling down over and over again, a hundred times. Perhaps he would remain quietly on his knees, his mind caught up in wonder, and this sometimes lasted a long time. Sometimes it seemed from the very way he looked that he had penetrated heaven in his mind, and then he would suddenly appear radiant with joy, wiping away the abundant tears running down his face.

Fifth Way of Prayer: Earnest Contemplation. Sometimes, when he was in a priory, our holy father Dominic would stand upright before the altar, not leaning on anything or supported by anything, but with his whole body standing erect on his feet. Sometimes he would hold his hands out, open, before his breast, like an open book, and then he would stand with great reverence and devotion, as if he were reading in the presence of God. At such times he seemed to be meditating, savoring the words of God. . .

Sixth Way of Prayer: Arms Outstretched. Sometimes, as I was told personally by someone who had seen it, our holy father Dominic was also seen praying with his hands and arms spread out like a cross, stretching himself to the limit and standing as upright as he possibly could. This was how the Lord prayed when he hung on the cross, his hands and arms stretched out, when, with great cries and weeping, his prayer was heard because of his reverence (Heb 5:7).

Seventh Way of Prayer: Supplication. He was also often found stretching his whole body up towards heaven in prayer, like a choice arrow shot straight up from a bow (Isa 49:2). He had his hands stretched right up above his head, joined together or slightly open as if to catch something from heaven. At such times the Holy Father seemed suddenly to enter the Holy of Holies and the third heaven (2 Cor 12:2). And so, after this kind of prayer, he bore himself like a prophet, as is related in his miracles, whether he was rebuking or dispensing or preaching.

Eighth Way of Prayer: Reading the Word. The Holy Father Dominic also had another beautiful way of praying, full of devotion and grace. After the canonical hours and the grace which is said in common after meals the father would go off quickly to some place where he could be alone, in a cell or somewhere. Sober and alert and anointed with a spirit of devotion which he had drawn from the words of God which had been sung in choir or during the meal, he would settle himself down to read or pray, recollecting himself in himself and fixing himself in the presence of God. Sitting there quietly, he would open some book before him, arming himself first with the sign of the cross, and then he would read. And he would be moved in his mind as delightfully as if he heard the Lord speaking to him

Ninth Way of Prayer: Praying Always. He also used to observe this way of prayer when he was going from one country to another, especially when he was in a lonely place. He disported himself with his meditations, in a state of contemplation. He would say to his travelling companions, 'It is written in Hosea, "I will lead her to a lonely place and speak to her heart"' (Hos 2:14). Sometimes he went aside from his companion or went on ahead or, more likely, lingered far behind; going on his own he would pray as he walked, and a fire was kindled in his meditation (Ps 38:4).[6]

DOMINIC SPEAKS

Dominic's Last Will and Testament

My dearest children, I have no earthly goods to leave you, because, as you know well, I have renounced all things; but I leave you something of greater worth, that is to say, the blessing of God and my own. I pray you, and as far as possible, command you to love one another and to remain always united having your hearts and wills conformable to that which Our Savior has taught you and which our Holy Rule imposes upon you and of which our Constitutions remind you. Do not allow yourselves to be made vain by any grace whatsoever God may bestow on you, whether temporal or spiritual, but with profound humility seek to recognize the obligation under which His benefits place you, which with the same humility you should endeavor to preserve. . .

The goods which I leave you, oh my children, are not gold and silver, treasures or other temporal wealth. They are the treasures of eternal salvation; the wealth of heaven; divine merchandise and an inheritance which ends not at death.

6. Tugwell, *Nine Ways of Prayer of Saint Dominic*, 15–46.

I leave you first, Charity, the eldest daughter of the grace of God. With this gift, you will be zealous in the service of God, ardent in promoting the salvation of your neighbor, and never among yourselves will discords and dissensions arise. Charity will unite you to God, and you will receive therefrom those favors which the true friends of God are accustomed to enjoy. In persecutions you will be intrepid, and many of you will not hesitate to shed your blood for the faith.

I leave you, secondly, Humility. She is so pleasing to God that for her He descended to earth and enclosed Himself in the Virgin's womb, beholding "the humility of His handmaiden." With this gift, if it continues with you, you shall be well pleasing to God and He will bestow on you His grace. By this virtue you will endear yourselves also to those around you, who, seeing in you that gentleness and patience which are the fruits of humility and considering the many services that you render them, will, in return, be unable to do less than love and assist you. Humility will remove from your heart all false pretension, free from all proud ambitions and relieve them of the heavy weight of temporal dignities. Through her you will become receptive of much divine light whereby to obtain a true understanding of the Holy Scriptures and great freedom and finally, you will enjoy great tranquility and peace, since he who is humble performs more willingly the will of another than his own. Cultivate, therefore, this holy virtue.

Lastly, I leave you Voluntary Poverty, that which, although she may indeed appear less comely outwardly, yet is the more fair and precious interiorly and well endowed with spiritual wealth, since it is certain that her merit cannot be paid with the price of this earth, and therefore is the Kingdom of Heaven assigned as her reward. By this virtue you will be liberated from all the entanglements of worldly interests and set loose towards all cares of this earth and towards all temporal affections. By her aid you will be exemplary in preaching and in the ministry of the Church. By her will you be loosed from earth and tend upward toward the sky. Be not disturbed if through poverty you shall find yourselves in manifest necessities, because the Heavenly Father, Who loves you more than any father whatsoever, will soon provide with generous hand nor will He who feeds the humblest beast of the earth suffer them to die of hunger who faithfully serve Him.[7]

7. Dominic, "Last Will and Testament."

QUESTIONS FOR REFLECTION

1. Dominic saw a close correlation between his message and his lifestyle. How do things match up for you, in this regard?
2. Dominic preferred an approach to the Cathars based on service and humility, not violent confrontation, condescension or an inquisitional manner. In what ways do you engage with those in your community who adopt a different attitude to you on crucial issues of the day?
3. Dominic was concerned that his religious brothers and sisters balanced study and service. He was more bookish than Francis, who famously wrote to Anthony of Padua: "It pleases me that you should teach sacred theology to the brothers as long as—in the words of the rule—you 'do not extinguish the spirit of prayer and devotion with study of this kind.'" How is your ministry or service underpinned and supported by study and learning? Recall also Dominic's action with books during the famine!
4. Jim Wallis writes: "Personal piety has become an end in itself instead of the energy for social justice . . . .Prophetic spirituality will always fundamentally challenge the system at its roots and offer genuine alternatives based on values from our truest religious, cultural and political traditions."[8] How did Dominic achieve this? How do you?
5. It could be said that Dominic fulfilled Paul's maxim about being "all things to all people." (Look up 1 Cor 9:19–23). This doesn't mean trying to do things to please everyone, but has something to do with how we adapt approaches to different types of people, as Dominic spoke the language of the poor and the language of academia according to the context he found himself in. How do you understand this? Is it a flexibility of approach you find helpful, or not?
6. What resonances, parallels or contrasts do you see between this chapter's character and Francis of Assisi?

FURTHER READING

Bedouelle, Guy. *Saint Dominic: The Grace of the Word.* San Francisco: Ignatius, 1987.
Monschau, Michael. *Praying with Dominic.* Frederick, MD: The Word Among Us, 1995.
Tugwell, Simon. *Saint Dominic and the Order of Preachers.* Dublin: Dominican, 2001.

8. Wallis, *Soul of Politics,* 38, 47.

PART 2

Jewish Luminaries

Jewish poet c.1250 conversing with cleric and women, from Codex Manesse

4

Living Reverently

Judah of Regensburg (1150–217), Eleazar of Worms (1176–1238), Dulcea (c1115—1196)

In the twelfth and thirteenth centuries a remarkable movement bubbled up in the German Rhineland, embracing cities like Worms, Mainz, and Speyer—no doubt encountered by the earliest Franciscan missionaries.[1] Known as the Hasidic Ashkenaz (Pious Ones of Germany) it became a key element in Jewish mysticism and indeed the precursor of the entire Kabbalah movement within Judaism, and a distant antecedent of the Hasidim which was to explode in eighteenth century eastern Europe. It emphasized intense piety, combining emergent Kabbalistic ideas with ethical teachings. We will meet its founder Judah ben Samuel of Regensburg, Judah the Pious (1150–217) and his family member, Eleazar of Worms (1176–1238) who took forward his ideas and brought them to a wider world, together with Eleazar's wife, Dulcea. Scholar Jospeh Dan writes of this movement:

> The Hasidim bequeathed upon esoterically inclined thinkers of the Middle Ages a picture of a colorful, rich, and variegated divine world containing myriads of angels and secondary powers. . .The Ashkenazi Hasidim, in a manner hardly equaled by any other Jewish group, believed in divine providence and guidance of even the

1. Franciscans arrived in the Rhineland (western Germany) around the 1220s. By the 1230s, Franciscan friaries were established in key cities such as Cologne, Mainz, and Trier, important centers for their preaching, teaching, and missionary work.

> most minute details of the world. There is one divine master plan, which is revealed in everything that happens. . .Ashkenazi Hasidic esoteric theology, which developed just before and simultaneous with the early Kabbalah, proves that medieval Judaism was developing new theological and mystical approaches to confront medieval challenges of both a physical and an intellectual nature. . .it was but one example within Judaism of a search for new ideas, terms, and symbols with which to give expression to a powerful religious impulse.[2]

JUDAH OF REGENSBURG

Born in Speyer, in the heart of the Upper Rhine Valley, a major center of the Holy Roman Empire during the Middle Ages, Judah was descended from a venerable family of early kabbalists from Northern Italy that had settled in Germany. He was nurtured in mystical prayer by his father Samuel ben Kalonymus, who has left us this hymn, "The Song of Unity":

> Everything is in You
>   and You are in everything
> You fill everything and you encompass it all;
> When everything was created,
>   You were *in* everything;
> Before everything was created,
>   You *were* everything.[3]

About 1195 Judah left his native place and settled in Regensburg (Ratisbon), probably to avoid localized persecution of Jews. Establishing himself in Bavaria on the Danube River, Judah became the towering figure of the Hasidic Ashkenaz, founding a *yeshiva* which flourished with many pupils earnestly thirsting for a more experiential approach to their faith. His work, the *Sefer Hasidim* represents the most important extant document of medieval Judaism and a milestone within Jewish literature, revealing fresh forms of devotion and mystical prayer. Judah conceived of a "new community" of pious Jews, with social interactions based on strict ethical principles. The *Sefer Hasidim* became the foundational ethical and mystical text in Ashkenazi Judaism, advocating humility, fear of God, poverty (material or

2. Dan, *Early Kabbalah*, 20, 21, 23.
3. Caravella, *Mystic Heart*, ch. 9: Middle Ages: Hasidei Ashkenaz.

spiritual), and high standards of moral conduct. It begins with a simple statement:

> This is called "Book of the Pious." Its contents are sweet and most desirable. It is written for those who fear God and revere his name. There is a *Hasid* [holy one] whose heart desires the love of his Creator, to do His will completely. But he does not know which matters to assume, which matters to avoid, or how to immerse himself thoroughly to do his Creator's will. The reason is that hearts have become deficient. There is a *Hasid* who undertakes a great deal and there is one who does little, but if he knew and understood matters of piety he would do a great deal more than those who do much. It is for this reason that the *Book of the Pious* was written, so that all who fear God and those returning to their Creator with a sincere heart may see, know, and understand all that they must do and all that they must avoid.[4]

These sayings give us a flavor of his teaching:

> Do not take pride in your wisdom. . . Pride is the root of many sins.
> A person may appear righteous before others, but if one's heart is proud and one's deeds are done to gain honor, they are counted among the wicked. . .
> Give charity in secret . . . It is better to give a small amount in humility than a large amount in arrogance.
> The tongue is more dangerous than the sword. . .
> The righteous person considers even the needs of his beast. . .
> Even if you have committed great sins. . . God receives you with love.[5]

The *Sefer Hasidim* describes within its parables and homilies the daily lives of medieval Jews under Christian rule, appealing to the everyday experiences of its audience. As a result, the text teems with clues about the religious and cultural landscape of Europe in the Middle Ages. Caravella writes:

> Not least significant are its detailed descriptions of the encounters between Jews and Christians. Although written in the wake of the Crusades, *Sefer Hasidim* attests to a surprising range of contacts between Jews and Christians, spanning the continuum from their common participation in a shared cultural context to their interpersonal interactions, both polemical and routine. In effect, this

4. Caravella, *Mystic Heart*, ch. 9.
5. Margaliot, *Sefer Ha-razim*, 104, 112, 393, 560, 666, 35.

> book preserves a poignant snapshot of a pivotal stage in the history of Jewish-Christian relations in Europe.[6]

The *Sefer Hasidim* opens a spiritual path of love for the Creator that is for many—these *Hasidim* did not see themselves as an aristocratic elite of scholars or spiritual leaders like the early kabbalists of southern Europe. But it describes a demanding and disciplined way of life for those seeking a more committed spiritual lifestyle and practice. Judah died in 1217, succeeded by his disciple and relative, Eleazar of Worms, who had been a member of his *yeshiva*.

ELEAZAR THE PERFUMER (1176–1238)

The teachings of Rabbi Judah and the Hasidic Ashkenaz were made more public by Eleazar. He became known as the *Roke'ah,* meaning "merchant of perfumes and medicines"—an allusion to how his mystical knowledge can perfume and heal the soul. All his writings are permeated by the scent of the sacred: his legacy embraces a voluminous literature codifying the Hasidic mystical doctrines, as well as works of religious law, commentary, poetry, and guidance for daily life. One key text is *Sefer HaRokeach,*[7] blending *halakah* (Jewish law), *mussar* (ethics) and *Kabbalah*:

> When you repent out of love, your sins become merits.
> Fear Heaven in private and in public, for the eyes of God are everywhere.
> Even when alone, you must conduct yourself with modesty, for the Shekhinah is with you.
> Suffering comes not to destroy but to purify, to elevate the soul like gold in the fire.
> Greater is one who gives in secret than one who offers public gifts.
> The deed without the heart is like a body without a soul.[8]

To subsequent generations Eleazar became known for his "magical" writings. His five-volume *Sefer Sodei Razaya* (*Secret of Secrets* or *Secrets of Reziel*) includes the section called *Sefer ha-shem* (*Book of the Holy Name*), explaining the secrets of using holy names of God. He believed that the messianic age would begin imminently, and that the Jews needed to be

6. Caravella, *Mystic Heart*, ch 9.
7. Hershler, *Sefer HaRokeach.*
8. Hershler, *Sefer Rokeach*, 26, 11, 35, 50, 84, 19.

ready for it, spurring him to make the esoteric teachings he had inherited through his lineage available to a wider audience. Caravella tells us about the transmission of ideas:

> Some of Rabbi Eleazar's students traveled south and came in contact with mystics in Provence and Spain and in turn transmitted the teachings to them. According to legend, Eleazar himself miraculously appeared in Spain at the end of his life to bring the secret wisdom of mystical prayer to Nachmonides (Moses ben Nahman), an important Spanish kabbalist of the Gerona school, thus acting as a link in the chain of transmission of the esoteric teachings from Aaron of Baghdad through the Kalonymides, from Italy to Germany and France, and then to Spain, where they merged with other influences to create the mystical teachings of the early kabbalists.[9]

Eleazer established himself at Worms, 30 miles from Bingen where Hildegard had recently flourished. He found himself living in a world where holiness and horror walked hand in hand, where the Jewish soul clung to its God amid sword, fire, and exile. To know Eleazar is to peer into a world of trembling awe and radiant flame. He was no philosopher of the ivory tower, but a mystic of blood and fire, of whispered names and midnight prayers, inheritor of a secret tradition passed from sage to sage. He saw the world as charged with spiritual energy, each act resonating through the heavens. In his eyes, God was terrifyingly near: a King wrapped in infinite mystery, yet responsive to the sighs of the broken-hearted. Eleazar wrote of the divine names, of angels who weep and watch, of the soul's longing to be rejoined with its Source. His mystical theology celebrated a vision of the universe woven from divine mercy and judgment, where humanity stood fragile before an overwhelming God, yet bound to Him in covenant and yearning.

Formative Suffering

Eleazar's mystical visions were not born in serenity. They were cries from the depths. In 1196, marauders descended upon Worms. They slaughtered his wife, Dulcea, and two of his daughters before his eyes, while he, wounded and bloodied, survived. In the aftermath, his writings became more piercing, more sorrowful, more aflame with longing. He poured his

9. Caravella, *Mystic Heart,* ch.9.

grief into *selichot* (penitential prayers), elegies, and mystical hymns: tears became theology.

He taught that life itself was a sanctuary, that one must live as if walking always before the Divine Presence, clothed in humility, immersed in prayer, purified by suffering. The commandments were not duties but doorways into holiness, into union with God.

He believed that even in exile, even in horror, the Jewish people could reach the Divine, through tears, through Torah, through trembling awe. His world was haunted by death but sustained by a terrible and beautiful hope: that from ashes could rise a prayer that touches heaven.

Names and Letters

Eleazar's mystical writings anticipated later Kabbalism and laid its foundations: such as the emphasis on the divine names, *sefirot* (divine emanations) and the power of language and letters. He developed ideas inherited from *Hekhalot* literature, a collection of early Jewish mystical texts from Late Antiquity and the early Middle Ages that describes ascents through heavenly "palaces" (*Hekhalot*) and visions of God's throne-chariot (*Merkabah*, from Ezekiel 1), symbol of *kavod*, the divine glory. So Eleazar represents a bridge between earlier Jewish mysticism and the more systematized Kabbalah. He wrote extensively on the mystical power of the Hebrew alphabet, viewing letters as channels of divine energy. He believed that by meditating on the divine names and manipulating letter combinations, one could connect with spiritual realms: the core idea of *gematria* that appears more fully developed in Kabbalah, seeing in every Hebrew syllable a symbolic meaning. Through his surviving texts, Eleazar still whispers to the wounded: "The soul is full of love of God and bound with ropes of love, in joy and lightness of heart. . .When the soul thinks deeply about the fear of God, then the flame of heartfelt love bursts in it and the exultation of innermost joy fills the heart."[10]

DULCEA (C1115–1196)

Though women's voices are rarely heard in this period, Eleazar's moving poetic lament over Dulcea's martyrdom points to their role as models of

10. Quoted by Scholem, *Jewish Mysticism*, 95.

a lived spirituality. Dulcea fulfilled the meaning of her name (gracious, pleasant), practicing and embodying his ideas, and his elegy celebrates the beating heart of a woman committed to the life of holiness. She walked the talk. Somehow she combined the role of wife and mother with that of businesswoman, women's leader of prayers in the synagogue she attended twice daily, and managing a household which welcomed (and fed) hungry students. The daughter of a cantor, she found time to teach singing and crafts, which included care and repair of the precious Torah scrolls. These were formative years for Eleazer, and we can only wonder how her faith and conversations with him shaped his own understanding and evolving ideas. Eleazar's tribute to her celebrates the life of faith, lived with dedication and humility. It was, after all, her selflessness which enabled the men to study and write! It is composed in the form of an alphabetic acrostic fashioned after Solomon's "Woman of Valor" in Proverbs 31.

> A woman of valor, her husband's crown, a daughter of aristocrats,
> A Godfearing Woman, renowned for her good deeds;
> Her husband trusts her implicitly, she fed and clothed him in dignity
> so he could sit among the elders of the land, and provide Torah study and good deeds;
> She always treats him well throughout their life together;
> Her labor provides him with books, her very name means "pleasant";
> She looked for white wool with which to make *tsitsit* [fringes of prayer shawl],
> she spun with enthusiasm;
> She foresees how to do many commandments, all who see her praise her;
> She is like the merchant ships: she feeds her husband so he can study Torah;
> Daughters saw her and declared her happy, her wares were so fine;
> She gives food to her household, and bread to the boys;
> How her hands held the distaff to spin cords for binding books;
> Zealous in everything she did, she spun cords for sewing *tefillin* [phylacteries]
> and for stitching together Torah scrolls;
> Quick as a deer she cooks for the young men and attends to the students' needs;
> She girded her loins with strength, and sewed some forty Torah scrolls;
> She prepared the feast, set the table for all the Fellows;

She adorned brides in good taste and brought them in honor;
"Pleasant" would bathe the dead, sew their shrouds;
Her hands sewed the students' clothes and torn books;
See how she distributes the fruits of her labor among Torah scholars;
She extends a hand to the poor, feeding her boys, daughters and husband;
She freely did the will of her Creator, day and night;
Her lamp will not go out in the night—
she makes wicks for the synagogue and schools:
She says Psalms; she sings hymns and prayers, she recites petitions;
Daily she says confession, and the Ten Commandments;
In all the towns she taught women so that they can chant songs;
She knows the order of the morning and evening prayers,
and she comes early to synagogue, stays late;
She stands throughout Yom Kippur, sings and prepared the candles beforehand;
She honors the Sabbaths and Holidays as well as Torah scholars;
She opens her mouth with wisdom,
On the Sabbath she sits and listens to her husband's sermon;
More modest than everyone, she is wise and faithful—
one is fortunate to be in her company;
When doing all the commandments she is zealous, selfless, gracious;
She bought milk for the students and hired them tutors from her earnings;
Known and wise, she serves her Creator joyfully.
She ran to visit the sick,to fulfill her Creator's commandments;
And she feeds her boys, nudges them to study, and serves the Name,
may He be blessed, out of proper fear;
"Pleasant" are her deeds; may the Hidden Rock remember her;
May her soul be adorned, bound in the bond of the light of the eternally living;
Give her of the fruit of her hands in Eden.[11]

ELEAZAR SPEAKS

Our extract for Eleazar comes from his "Book of Unity", part of *The Book of the Secrets of Reziel (Sefer Sodei Razaya).*

11. Marcus, "Mothers, Martyrs, and Moneymakers".

I am writing this book[12] to proclaim the secrets and reveal the strength of the Creator of the universe. Humanity is happy to learn the secrets. Revere the Lord. Know of the unity of God. Give your heart over to reverence. Bow down to him. He is one and there are not two of him. Blessed is he. He is first and last. He is King over all the universe. There is no other unto him. The Lord alone is sublime.

Blessed are the wise by the mysteries coming from the wisdom of the Torah, given to teach the truth of reverence to human beings. Honor the strength and glory of the *Shekinah*. The secret word is as milk and honey upon the tongue. Let it be to you alone. The teachings are not foreign to you. This book proclaims the secret of Reziel, but only to the humble. Stand in the middle of the day, without provocation and without reward. Learn the tributes of the reverence of God. Turn away from evil and journey on the path to pursue righteousness. The secret is reverence of the Lord. The worthy go directly to the secret. The beginning of wisdom is reverence of the Lord: rejoice and build the house of wisdom with the secret of this foundation. Be wise by opening the heart to the secret.

Show reverence to the heavens all the day. Regard love in the heart. The reverence of the heavens is in the heart at all times, reverence of the purity of the Lord. Those giving reverence are loved by the Lord.

There is much value in living in purity. Bathe in the glory of the light of God. Go from darkness into light, separated from those led astray. As the light shines down upon the sea, that is the reverence of God who spoke to Abraham, beloved of God. From love, understanding was created by the love and reverence. A thousand generations come after from the love.

The God and Father and King is strong and wise, good and compassionate.

O God, you tolerate all things, filling all the highest and lowest, sustaining in the high places and bringing forth all creatures. You reveal the mysteries of the universe, the knowledge of good and evil. You tolerate wickedness for the sake of the restoration.

Behold, all goodness to the righteous who love God. Give praise and laud over the greatest works. Bow down in supplication and petition. Petition for every measure of goodness for the sake of the benefit of the body. This is the foundation of wisdom, understanding of knowledge. From this, bring light into your days. Give reverence and serve God in great fear. Receive salvation

12. Traditionally reporting what Adam revealed to Reziel, angel of God's mystery. Savedow, *Book of the Angel Reziel*, 34.

from affliction, injury, and suffering. Do not writhe in pain. Do not bring death or speak evil. Fill your days with goodness and blessings in the world.

The beginning of wisdom is reverence of the Lord and love of heaven. The heart of the righteous burns as flames of fire. Keep the commandments in reverence of the Lord. This the Lord God requires, not making reward for reverence and love. Fall down in supplication and cry out to God. Show reverence in prayer and receive tranquility therein. Avoid all evil. Dwell in the secret place of the Most High, hidden in the darkness of the shadow of God. Wherefore be silent, and bring forth from the secret place what the Father reveals to you.

The universe is treasured by God as the measure of heaven. Speak of heaven. Proclaim the praise, saying: Praised is the Ruler above. Prayers proclaim the glory. By prayer, stay upon the path of the Lord. At first, the *Shekinah* precedes the universe by myriad myriads of years. The glory of the universe is above or below, deep and profound. It is in the east and west, north and south. How great is the light!

Also, make clear the reverence of God. We serve God with love in the heart. Great is the reverence and devotion. Establish the heart. Keep the commandments. Rejoice in supplication to serve the Creator of the universe. By rejoicing and reverence, serve the Lord in holy fear and tremble in exaltation. It is written, serve the Lord by rejoicing. The heart rejoices to petition the Lord. Uphold the reverence of God, not to fall from grace. In every place, revere God and serve in reverence and love. Be sustained in exaltation by the reverence of God. Bringing peace in the world, serve from love and supplication, and strengthen the body. Serving in reverence is the foundation. At this time, become wise and prosper. Of the love of the blessed, after, write the secret of the *Merkabah* [chariot/divine throne]. Be wise by reverence forever.

The King of all kings, God, exalts in reverence before going on all paths. The Lord is everywhere and in every place. He observes the good and wicked in every place. The worthy revere the Lord in righteousness. Unite the nations. Work for the sake of the heavens. God's blessings open up every path. God gives life to you in the heart. By the path of reverence, reveal all thoughts and understanding of all works. Rise up that these words may come true.[13]

13. Savedow, trans. *The Book of the Angel Reziel,* Part 1:1.

QUESTIONS FOR REFLECTION

1. What is the relationship, do you think, between prayerful living and spiritual disciplines?
2. What can you learn from the faithfulness of Dulcea?
3. What lines strike you most forcibly from the extracts?
4. What are the signs of reverence in your life? How does it reveal itself in your attitudes to people, things and planet? How can you foster a sense of awe as you go through each day?
5. What resonances, parallels or contrasts do you see between this chapter's characters and Francis of Assisi?

FURTHER READING

Baskin, Judith R. "Dolce of Worms: The Lives and Deaths of an Exemplary Medieval Jewish Woman and her Daughters" in *Judaism in Practice: From the Middle Ages through the Early Modern Period*, edited by Lawrence Fine, 429–37. Princeton, NJ: Princeton University Press, 2001. (Includes English translations of all of the documents related to Dulcea and a discussion of Dulcea's activities).

Dan, Joseph and Grozinger, Karl, eds. *Mysticism, Magic, and Kabbalah in Ashkenazi Judaism*. New York: Walter De Gryter, 1995.

Kanarfogel, Ephraim. *Peering Through the Lattices: Mystical, Magical, and Pietistic Dimensions in the Tosafist Period.* Detroit, Michigan: Wayne State University Press, 2000.

Sharma, Arvind, ed. *Women Saints in World Religions.* Albany, NY: SUNY, 2000.

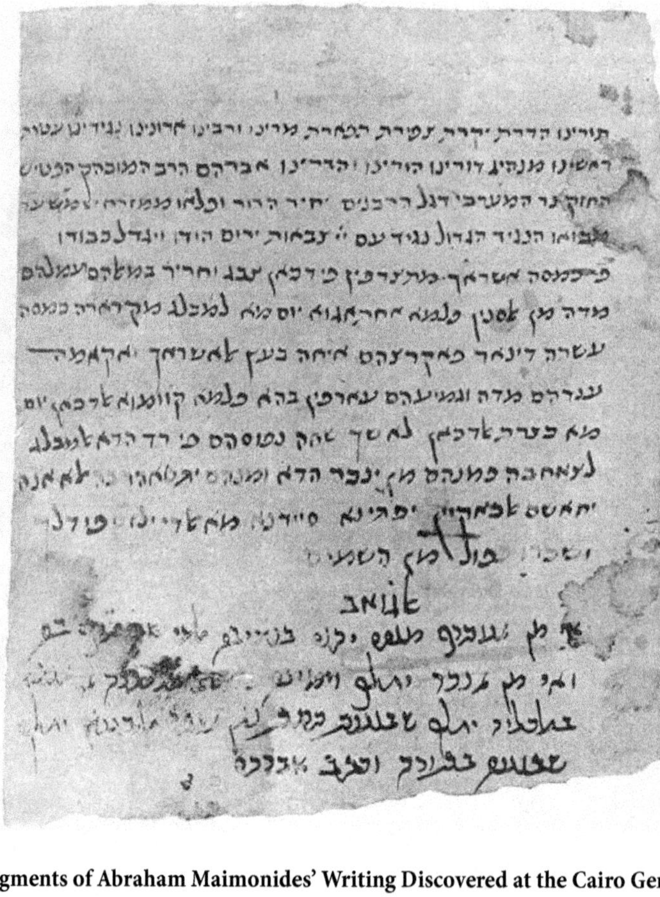

Fragments of Abraham Maimonides' Writing Discovered at the Cairo Genizah

5

Living Purposefully

Abraham Maimonides (1186–1237)

We would know little about the teaching of Abraham Maimonides were it not for an astonishing discovery of a vast cache of ancient Jewish texts that was stumbled upon late in the nineteenth century.

The indominable Scottish twin sisters and scholars Agnes S. Lewis and Margaret D. Gibson, who also discovered Syriac manuscripts at Sinai[1], returned to Cambridge in 1896 from Egypt bearing outstanding parchments, books and ancient letters from the Cairo Genizah, a hidden horde of some 400,000 Jewish manuscript fragments housed haphazardly in a storeroom of the 11th century Ben Ezra Synagogue in Old Cairo. Given the "tip-off" and led to this treasure trove by Cambridge friend and rabbi-scholar Solomon Schechter, they had managed to climb a steep ladder high up from the women's gallery and through a window. It was akin to Howard Carter's discovery of Tutankhamun's tomb and his *eureka* exclamation "Everywhere the glint of gold!"—except this was high up in the roof and pile upon pile of precious manuscripts and scrolls were covered with thick layers of dust! In Jewish tradition, it is inappropriate to throw away documents bearing the divine Name, so over centuries they had been thrown into this depository, the high window acting as kind of postbox. These manuscripts, written on vellum, paper and papyrus, spanning the entire period of Middle-Eastern, North African, and Andalusian Jewish history between the 6th and 19th

1. Soskice, *Sisters of Sinai.*

centuries, turned out to be the largest and most diverse collection of medieval manuscripts in the world! Among the texts was found a draft copy, in his own hand, of Moses Maimonides' *Guide for the Perplexed* and substantial portions of Abraham Maimonides' *A Comprehensive Guide for the Servants of God,* a practical and spiritual manual for those seeking a life of devotion.

The rediscovery of Abraham Maimonides' writings has challenged the common narrative that Jewish mysticism emerged mostly from Kabbalah in Spain and Provence, showing that a parallel stream of Jewish Sufism flourished in the Islamic East. It has elevated Abraham from a footnote in history to major thinker in Jewish intellectual history. It has revealed an interfaith dialogue in practice: Jewish thinkers deeply engaging with Muslim spiritual traditions while maintaining a strong Jewish identity.

Written in Judeo-Arabic (Arabic in Hebrew script), his *Guide for the Servants of God* describes pathways to holiness and perfection. What is striking is that the specific virtues he identifies—sincerity, mercy, generosity, gentleness, humility, trust in God, contentedness, chastity, fighting against one's nature, control of human faculties to serve their high ends, and solitude—are all paralleled in the path of the Sufi in practically the same sequence and are called by almost the same names. Though steeped in Hebrew spirituality, Abraham reveals a remarkable openness to other pathways: indeed, he stands out as an exemplar one prepared to learn from and even appropriate Islamic practices while upholding the integrity of his own tradition. How did he come to be so influenced by the Sufi tradition, and end up as counsellor to Francis' friend Malek al-Kamil?

Born in 1186, Abraham Maimonides was the son of the famous Sephardic theologian and legal authority Moses Maimonides, regarded by many as the greatest Jewish philosopher of the Middle Ages.

The Father

Moses Maimonides (1138–1204) had been born in Cordoba, a thriving center of Jewish learning and Islamic culture. After being persecuted by the puritanical Almohads (Berber Muslim Caliphate) during a time of great political upheaval in Spain, Maimonides and his family fled to Fez in Morocco. He went on to become a great leader of the Jewish community in Egypt, based in Old Cairo. Because rabbis were not paid in that time, he trained to become a physician, quickly rising to be one of the most influential physicians of his time, becoming at 18 official doctor to the court of Saladin, ruler of Egypt and uncle of Malek al-Kamil.

He wrote major essays on Jewish law, the most famous being *The Guide for the Perplexed,* reconciling rational philosophy with religious faith. Living in the religious melting pot of North Africa, Moses Maimonides was hugely influenced by all the faiths surrounding him as he explored Arab and Greek ideas. His own teachings also influenced the non-Jewish world during that period, and Christian leaders such as Thomas Aquinas (1225–1274) referred to him in writings as "Rabbi Moses." Bringing four cultures—Greco-Roman, Arab, Jewish, and Western—together in one person, he remains one of the most influential religious philosophers of the intellectual world.[2]

Moses Maimonides saw great promise in his exceptionally gifted child:

> Of the affairs of this world I have no consolation, save in two things: preoccupation with my studies and the fact that God has bestowed upon my son Abraham, grace and blessings similar to those he gave to him whose name he bears [i.e. the Patriarch Abraham] . . . for, in addition to his being meek and humble towards his fellow men, he is endowed with excellent virtues, sharp intelligence and a kind nature. With the help of God, he will certainly gain renown amongst the great. . .[3]

The Son

After his father's death in 1204, Cairo-born Abraham succeeded him at the age of 18 as the head of Egyptian Jewry. He served as both religious and political leader (*Nagid*), a position he held for over three decades. Abraham continued his father's rationalist tradition but also incorporated more mystical and pietistic elements into his thought. As we shall see, he was influenced by the Islamic mysticism of Sufism and integrated some of its practices into Jewish pietism. Like his father, Abraham was a prominent physician and served in the palaces of the Ayyubid rulers of Egypt, becoming physician in the court of Malek al-Kamil—an important relationship giving unparalleled access to the Sutan who so influenced and respected St Francis in their 1219 encounter. It is quite possible that ideas from Abraham

2. See Mayes, *Gateways to the Divine.*
3. Maimonides, *Epistulae,* "Letter to Joseph ben Judah", 96.

featured in the Sutan's extended conversation with Francis, suggesting a tantalizing but unprovable chain of influence.

Abraham Maimonides is notable for blending rationalism with mysticism. While his father explored the interplay between Aristotelian rationalism and Jewish law, Abraham delighted in spiritual experience, ethical self-refinement, and mystical devotion. Paul Fenton, leading scholar of the era, insightfully states that Abraham moved from his father's prescriptive mode to a descriptive mode explaining the spiritual significance of Judaism in the same manner as al-Ghazali did for Islam. He promoted meditative prayer, inner purity, and practices resembling Sufi rituals, though always within a Jewish framework. His pietistic movement, sometimes called the Jewish-Sufi movement, had influence for generations in Egypt and beyond. He is considered one of the last great figures of medieval Judeo-Arabic culture. Tom Block observes:

> Abraham grew up in a truly multi-cultural world, where Moslems, Jews and even Christians interacted in one of the most accepting societies in the history of humanity. Medieval Egypt was a place of mutual respect, protective laws and surprisingly strong and positive relations between the religions. It was also a time and place rife with Sufis and Sufi thought—and Jewish libraries often contained books by such masters as al-Ghazali, as-Suhrawardi and al-Hallaj, all dutifully transcribed into the blocky Hebrew script of the local Jewish population. Sufis and Jews knew each other, read each other's books and even compared notes on spirituality and the quest for divine union with God.[4]

What Are We Aiming At?

In *A Comprehensive Guide for the Servants of God* Abraham sets before his readers a vision of the objective of the spiritual life—*wusul ila Llah* meaning "arriving at God", reaching the ultimate goal of human existence. This concept reflects the Sufi influence on his thought, where *wusul* signifies not just knowledge *about* God, but an existential nearness or union with the Divine Presence. It goes beyond intellectual knowledge (as in his father's rationalism) and implies a transformational closeness to God. It suggests a journey or path (*tariq*) toward the divine presence. Perfection, in this view,

4. Block, "Abraham Maimonides: A Jewish Sufi".

is not static—it is a process, spiritual *paths* or *wayfaring* culminating in arrival. Rosenblatt observes of the *summum bonum*:

> The end in view in perfecting the soul is to arrive at the *wusul*—the highest kind of perfection attainable by humanity. This is defined as a clinging to God: the person's thoughts are entirely wrapt up in God and one is liberated from and forgets about everything else, which effect is brought about by dedicating all our faculties to God, by using our reason to acquire the knowledge that would aid us in comprehending God's existence and by sincerely loving God and being present before God. Renouncing this world is equivalent with union with God. Again *wusul* is interpreted as denoting being near to God, meeting God, being seen by God, seeing God, knowing God, comprehending God's greatness—an excellence enduring in this world as well as the world to come—speaking to God in a prophetic vision, attaining the "spirit of holiness" and praising God while one is under its influence. This is also called "bliss," and one form of such complete spiritual delight one acquires by lingering in the Temple (Ps 27:4).[5]

In order to unfold and develop the soul's spiritual potential both theoretical study and practical training are necessary. Abraham delineates complementary and essential pathways we must take: "the high ways," or "ways of the heart". We can gauge our progress according to the distance we have covered in this journey, which should not be undertaken without a mentor. In a moment, we shall let Abraham speak to us of three pathways: generosity, gentleness and solitude. First, let's consider the influence of Sufi mysticism on his thought.

Sufi Ideas Meet Jewish

In fact, at this time piety and spirituality in medieval Jewish culture of the Near East and North Africa were saturated with the core ideals of Sufism. The idea that the individual ought to pursue an inner path to communion with God, the ascetic emphasis on elevating the spirit over bodily desires, the practice of regular fasting and solitary prayer—these were widely cherished ideals among religious groups of the medieval Islamic world. Abraham Maimonides proposed changes to synagogue practice to enhance piety and bring the service more in line with Islamic piety. These practices

5. Rosenblatt, *High Ways Vol 1*, 95–98.

include the washing of hands and feet before prayer, kneeling in synagogue and arrangement in orderly rows like in a mosque, full prostration (Jewish custom is to bow), and prostration at the end of every Psalm and raising one's hands heavenward at the start of each paragraph.

In a major new study Elisha Russ-Fishbane affirms:

> Islam was, paradoxically, essential to Abraham Maimonides' vision of Judaism. Make no mistake, this was no postmodern vision of a pluralistic Judaism.
>
> For Abraham Maimonides, Judaism was at a crisis point, a spiritual nadir in its age-old exile. As he saw it, nothing short of a religious revival and a return to the abandoned roots of the religion could lift the Jews from the morass of exile and hasten the redemption. Abraham envisioned his brand of *hasidut [piety]* as an essential part of that revival.
>
> If Islam (Sufism included) had incorporated a number of those lost traditions, the path to Jewish revival—and the path to messianic redemption—required a profound engagement with the religion of Islam. The result was a unique combination of inner Jewish traditionalism and an openness to the wisdom of a foreign religion.[6]

His teaching on solitude is a case in point.

Abraham viewed solitude not as isolation for its own sake but as a disciplined practice for inner refinement. Solitude allowed the practitioner to withdraw from worldly distractions and focus entirely on divine contemplation and prayer. He identifies two expressions of *hitbodedut* or self-seclusion: *outward solitude* involves physical separation to eliminate distractions and quieten the senses, while *inward*, directing one's awareness ("heart and mind") away from worldly concerns ("all besides God") seeks to focus completely on God ("fill and occupy them with Him"). The bodily aspect of such seclusion serves as a route to the inner practice, which seeks to deepen *devekut*, attachment, cleaving to God, leading to the intimacy of encounter with God.

He believed that practicing solitude imitated the spiritual lives of the Hebrew prophets, particularly Moses, who frequently withdrew into the wilderness or into a tent to commune with God. Abraham connects this to the prophetic model of spiritual retreat as preparation for divine inspiration.

6. Russ-Fishbane, *Judaism, Sufism, and the Pietists*, 44.

This echoes Sufi concepts but is also rooted in Jewish notions of *hitbodedut*. Sufis valued solitude or retreat (*khalwa*) as a central practice to engender purification of the heart, remembrance of God (*dhikr*), and the mystical union with the Divine. They practiced isolation from society to intensify inner focus and achieve stages of mystical realization, but Abraham never advocated a monastic type of seclusion: like his father, he saw as important engagement with the world, family, and community. Solitude was meant to be temporary and purposeful, integrated into a larger ethical and religious life. He recommends practices like silent meditation, tears during prayer, and retreat into nature or a private room. His supplicatory prayers (*tahannunim*) done in private were inspired by the Sufic intimate discourses with God (*munajat*). Abraham Maimonides selectively incorporated Sufi methods, emphasizing those compatible with Jewish law. His descriptions of ideal prayer often mirror Sufi manuals.

ABRAHAM MAIMONIDES SPEAKS

The Elevated Paths

The elevated paths are bound up with one another and follow necessarily from one another. Mercy is bound up with generosity and with gentleness, and humility is bound up with contentedness, and faith in God. You find the merciful person to be generous; the gentle person is humble, and so forth. The reason for that is that these paths have, to begin with, one aim: "a good heart." All these paths lead to one end and that is the goal. Some of these elevated paths are qualities ascribed to God, exalted be He, like mercy and generosity and gentleness: (reflecting) the *imitatio Dei* to which we are summoned.

We are in the state of training in them, before they become fixed forms in the soul, as we approach nearer to the "goal" (*summum bonum*).

Set your heart and turn your care to what we explain about these elevated paths which are the purposes of the Law, as enlightenment with the help of heaven.

Generosity

Generosity is one of the elevated paths and one of the purposes of the Law and one of the attributes ascribed to God, exalted be He, for He is "gracious" and "abundant in kindness" (Exod 34:6). His bringing into existence the creation was an act of bounty and generosity: "The world is built out of kindness" (Ps 89:3). His liberality and His generosity embrace all His creatures: "The Lord is good to all" (Ps 145:9).

Generosity is an expression of lavish bestowal of benefits upon someone who does not have any claim upon it nor deserves it. Paying the hired man his wage and the creditor his debt is not generosity but righteousness and justice: charity to the poor, and hospitality, and gift-giving are generosity.

Now the generosity we are exhorted to consists in our being liberal toward our fellows—not in our being lavish toward ourselves only; on the contrary, if we are frugal with ourselves and liberal toward our fellows that would be an increase in our generosity. The generosity that is lauded does not consist in spending wealth upon another than ourselves in any way whatsoever, as the multitude understands generosity as meaning merely giving much food to whoever chances to come our way and the presenting of gifts to whoever is there. Rather the generosity we are exhorted to as one of the elevated paths consists in our being generous and liberal with the resources God has given us toward any person who needs it.

So understand that and meditate about it. Now generosity with your wealth consists in you not hoarding that which God has given to you, nor in merely spending it on things superfluous to your sustenance or the upkeep of your family. Be liberal with it towards your fellow men and women, as the Law exhorts: "Rejoice in all the good the Lord your God has given you: you, and the Levite, and the stranger that is in the midst of you" (Deut 26:11).

There is a difference between the one who is generous with a well-visited banquet given to rich people who do not need it, and the one who with quantity feeds poor people who do need it. God said in respect to His attributes and His liberality: "To revive the spirit of the humble and to revive the heart of the contrite ones" (Isa 57:15). He said what he finds acceptable: "Is it not to deal your bread to the hungry, and to bring the poor, that are cast out, to your house? When you see the naked, cover him. . .Draw out your soul to the hungry, and satisfy the afflicted soul" (Isa 58:7,10). The generosity that we are exhorted to is not only generosity with wealth and what can be bought with it, also generosity with one's power, knowledge and religion. As for generosity with one's power it consists in being liberal with that whereof God, exalted be He, has given us.[7]

7. Rosenblatt, *High Ways Vol 1*. Ch. XV on Generosity, 169, 171, 173.

Gentleness

Gentleness is possible when wrath and anger are close to being absent; it is one of the elevated prophetic paths and one of the attributes ascribed to God, namely that God is "long-suffering." In this elevated path there *either* is in the constitution of the person and their nature a disposition for it by virtue of the equilibrium of the heart and the tranquility of the impulsive faculty and the abundance of the reasoning faculty, so that the training for it is easy; *or* there is in the person's character the difficulty of not being disposed for it owing to the person's being of a hot temperament and their impulsive faculty tending disposed to anger, so that only strenuous cultural and legal training can resist that disposition. As Solomon says: "The one who is slow to anger is better than the mighty; and the one who rules their spirit better than those who take a city" (Prov 16:32). This refers to those who have the power to control their wrath and to resist it.

The kind of gentleness that is lauded is due to the authority of the reasoning faculty over the impulsive faculty and its sovereignty over it, employing it according to the intellect and to the Law—not that that be due merely to coldness of temperament and the fatigue of the impulsive faculty and feebleness. Anger is the thing that incites to vengeance and for many leaves rancor behind in the soul. Now, if the anger be evident and strong and there be coupled with it the power to take revenge, then revenge takes place, just as kings and their ilk take revenge immediately in the moment of their wrath. But, if the anger be weak and hidden and coupled with powerlessness to take speedy revenge, it also leaves rancor behind in the soul. That's why the Bible couples the prohibition against the nursing of hatred with the prohibition against revenge-taking: "You shall not take vengeance nor bear any grudge." Anger is a consequence of ignorance and just as gentleness points to knowledge and the strength of mind. The two paths of gentleness and humility are associated, just as their two opposites anger and pride are associated, for what mostly arouses the impulsive faculty to anger is inner pride and what mostly brings about gentleness is inner humility. Therefore the sages, blessed be their memory, exhort strongly to this noble trait, saying: "A person should always be yielding like a reed and not unbending like a cedar. Therefore was the reed privileged to supply the pen with which to write the Torah."[8]

8. Rosenblatt, *High Ways Vol 1*. Ch. XVI on Gentleness, 183.

Solitude

Solitude is among the most distinguished of the elevated paths. It is moreover the way of the very great saints and by it the prophets achieved union with God. It may be divided into external solitude and internal solitude, and the aim of external solitude is the attainment of internal solitude which is the last rung of the rungs of the ladder leading us to union with God. By internal solitude is meant complete sincerity of heart, to attain what David prayed for: "Create in me a clean heart O God" (Ps 51:12). This consists in clearing the heart and the mind of everything except God, and of their being filled and inhabited by God. That comes about through the stillness of the sensitive part of the soul, and the withdrawal of the impulsive part from worldly things and its inclination towards God, and the preoccupation of the rational part of the soul with God, and the employment of the imaginative part in what supports the rational in the observation of His great creatures that indicate His existence, such as the observation of the majesty of the sea and its terror and the marvels of its living things, or the observation of the rotation of the sphere in all its magnificence and the nature of the stars and the like.

This path is the last of the elevated paths and is contiguous with mystic reunion with God. Both external solitude and internal solitude are a journey. . .[9]

QUESTIONS FOR REFLECTION

1. What stands out for you or strikes you from this text?
2. How do you respond to Maimonides' teaching on the relationship between anger and gentleness? Was Francis or Jesus ever angry? If so, why?
3. In what ways do you practice solitude?
4. How would you describe its benefits?
5. What resonances, parallels or contrasts do you see between this chapter's character and Francis of Assisi?

9. Rosenblatt, *High Ways Vol 2*. Chapter on Solitude, 383, 419.

FURTHER READING

Idel, M. et al, eds. *Jewish Mystical Leaders and Leadership in the 13th Century*. Lanham, Maryland: Jason Aronson Inc, 1998.

Maimonides, Obadyah [Abraham's son]. *The Treatise of the Pool: Al-Mawala Al Hawdiyya*. Translated by Paul Fenton, with useful introduction to Abraham. Cambridge, MA: Ishk, 1981.

Wieder, N. *Islamic Influences on the Jewish Worship*. Oxford: East and West Library, 1947.

Naçhmanides by Meir Kunstadt

6

Living Humbly

Nachmanides (1194–1270)

NACHMANIDES, KNOWN IN HEBREW as Rabbi Moshe ben Nachman, or by the acronym Ramban[1], was a mystic, jurist, and scholar of the Torah. Born in Girona, Catalonia, he lived during an age marked by clashes—and sometimes positive exchanges—between faiths echoing through the streets and synagogues of medieval Spain.

From a young age, Nachmanides possessed a soul ablaze. He was no dry academic but a man whose mind pulsed with the rhythms of revelation. A physician by trade and a sage by destiny, he devoured the Talmud and drank deeply from the early springs of *Kabbalah*.

Unlike Moses Maimonides, who sought to harmonize Judaism with Aristotelian philosophy, Nachmanides bristled at the cold rationalism of the Greek mind. For him, the Torah was not just a code of law or a philosophical riddle, but a living, breathing organism, shot through with divine sparks, a tapestry woven with cosmic secrets and sacred symbols. Drazin claims: "As a mystic, Nachmanides was the first person [in Judaism] to introduce the idea that the Torah contains mystical notions, and the first to offer a mystical interpretation of the Bible."[2] His exegesis is life-affirming and inspirational: "Nachmanides, the tender and compassionate,

1. also used of Moses Maimonides.
2. Drazin, *Unusual Thinker*, xviii.

represented Judaism from the side of emotion and feeling, as Moses Maimonides did from the side of reason and logic."[3]

He became one of the foremost scholars in reconquered Spain, leading large and influential Catalonian communities for most of his life. He wrote works of *halakah*, biblical commentary, and his most famous work *Commentary on the Torah* is still printed in nearly every Jewish Study Bible: here he combines mysticism, philosophy, medicine, and science in a comprehensive and contextual analysis of the text. Adlerblum avers:

> No sufficient place has been given to Nachmanides as a philosopher, and yet he is more original than the others. He took as his starting-point the facts of Judaism, including even the narratives of the Talmud. He diverted from the too-much-discussed problem of the relation of religion to reason, and turned his attention to the relation of religion to humanity. He tried to remove the antithesis between soul and body, and asserted that the contempt of flesh was inconsistent with religion. He upheld the doctrine of Judaism that we should rejoice on the day of joy, and weep on the day of sorrow.[4]

Nachmanides was a pioneer in kabbalistic thought and interpretation. Rabbi Dr Charles Chavel affirms that the "great kabbalist of the sixteenth century Isaac Luria spoke of Ramban's presentation of kabbalistic principles in the highest terms: 'Deep they lie, exceptionally deep; who can grasp them?'"[5]

Trial and Exile

Like Moses Maimonides Ramban was both a physician and a public figure, engaging in disputations and defenses on behalf of the Jewish community in the Christian courts of northern Spain.

It was in the heat of confrontation that Nachmanides' courage would truly shine. In 1263, at the age of 69, he was summoned by King James I of Aragon to Barcelona for a public disputation—Judaism vs. Christianity—with a man born Jewish but who converted to Christian faith, had become a priest and who wanted to prove that Jesus was indeed the long-awaited Messiah. They debated for four days, Ramban doing well, but then faced

3. Solomon Schechter, who we met in connection with the Cairo Genizah, in "Nachmanides".

4. Adlerblum, "Reinterpretation of Jewish Philosophy".

5. Chavel quoted in Drazin, *Unusual Thinker*, 4.

legal charges of blasphemy against him. Recognizing the danger, he left Spain to fulfill a life-long dream of moving to the land of Israel.

He sailed east and arrived in Acre, then a war-torn shell, a land aching with ruin under Crusader and Muslim strife. At the age of 72, he journeyed to Jerusalem, finding it severely depleted of its Jewish population, which in happier times had lived in peaceful co-existence with Muslims and Christians. He heartened the struggling Jewish presence by founding a substantial synagogue.[6]

Hidden Miracles

One of the key theological concepts he developed is the idea of "hidden miracles" which he distinguished from *open* or *revealed miracles* like the splitting of the Red Sea. Hidden miracles are divine interventions that appear to occur through natural processes. Unlike overt miracles, these are veiled within nature, so they can be perceived as coincidental or normal if one does not look deeply. Nachmanides argues, especially in his *Commentary on the Torah*

> From the great and public miracles, a person comes to recognize the hidden miracles . . . that everything is a miracle; there is no part of nature or the world that is independent.[7]

Ramban teaches that belief in the open miracles of the Exodus should lead a person to recognize God's hand in all aspects of life, even in what seems "natural." This means that everything is under divine control, whether it seems miraculous or not.

Hidden miracles are a test of faith. Since they are not obvious, recognizing them requires a deeper belief in God's ongoing involvement in the world. Nachmanides' view challenges the idea of an autonomous natural world. Instead, it emphasizes unbroken divine involvement. God manifests both through nature and above it.

Today, popular views of miracles persist in the attitude exemplified by 18th century David Hume's *Enquiry Concerning Human Understanding*: "A miracle is a violation of the laws of nature." They are an exception to the rule. But contemporary cosmology celebrates the fluidity and dynamic of

6. The Ramban Synagogue still stands in the Old City to this day. Destroyed in 1948 it was rebuilt and its distinctive dome restored in 2007.

7. Nachmanides, *Commentary*, Exod 13:16.

the universe: all is in a state of flux. Some would add: "God is ever-creative." Nachmanides teaches that everything in life, big or small, is miraculous, even if it seems ordinary. These "hidden miracles" are moments where God acts invisibly but purposefully. Open miracles (like the Exodus) are rare and public. Hidden miracles occur constantly—health, weather, livelihood, success—but appear natural. They teach us to live with faith, humility, and spiritual awareness, seeing divine intention in all things.

Divine Providence

Nachmanides develops a profound and spiritually charged doctrine of divine providence (*hashgacha*) that is one of the key pillars of his theological worldview. What appears as natural causality is often a hidden form of divine providence. Unlike Moses Maimonides who treats providence in a more rationalist and philosophical framework, Ramban argues for a more intimate, relational, and supernatural model of God's involvement in the world.

Nachmanides teaches that God governs the world through direct oversight, particularly over individuals who are close to Him (the righteous). "God only exercises Providence over those who are close to Him . . . But those who abandon Him are abandoned to the natural order."[8] The more faithful, righteous, or spiritually connected a person is, the more directly God's involvement becomes evident. So Nachmanides closely links providence to moral behavior. Righteous people are protected by providence, even through hidden miracles. Repentance and spiritual effort attract divine attention: "He who comes to purify himself is helped from Heaven."

But providence is not only about judgment or reward—it is also about divine presence (*Shekinah*) and spiritual alignment. Nachmanides was deeply influenced by early Kabbalah: God's providence flows through the *Sefirot*, divine channels of emanation. *Tzimtzum* (divine concealment—God, as it were, holding himself back) allows for hidden providence, where God appears absent but is secretly guiding events. Nachmanides' conception of God contains a dimension of transcendence, beyond human comprehension and expression. As he experimented with the language of the *Sefirot* Nachmanides expressed a distinction between two levels of divinity—the known and the unknown, reminiscent of Pseudo-Dionysius, the fifth century Christian Syrian writer.

8. Nachmanides, *Commentary*, Gen 18:19.

Living by Faith

Nachmanides offers a deeply spiritual and theologically rich view of living by faith, which integrates trust in God, recognition of his hidden involvement, awareness of the Divine. For Ramban, faith (*Emunah*) is not just abstract belief, but a living, continuous relationship with God, the lens through which one views all reality. Faith is recognizing God's presence in everything. Ramban insists that to live by faith means to believe that nothing is random or merely natural: everything is an expression of God's will. Ramban says that one must constantly look out for and discern God's hand at work in everything, even when events seem ordinary. This demands a worldview in which every breath, success, illness, or storm is God acting inwardly or outwardly. Living by faith means being spiritually alert, trained to perceive hidden miracles.

Ramban teaches that God's providence watches over the righteous, even if his actions seem hidden or painful. True faith isn't shaken by suffering. A believer sees meaning and purpose even in hardship, trusting that God's hand is guiding. Faith means believing in God's goodness even when outcomes are unclear. He experienced this for himself in his rejection at Barcelona and move to Palestine, affirming "He is close to those who are close to Him . . . and guides them with hidden kindness."[9]

Living by faith is not passive. Three things stand out. Faith expresses itself through *Mitzvot* (commandments): acts that demonstrate loyalty and connection to God. All *Mitzvot* are meant to cultivate a deep awareness and trust in God's presence, not just in belief, but in the lived experience of his closeness: "The goal of all the commandments is that we should believe in our God . . . and that we should trust in Him."[10]

Secondly, prayer is indispensable, understood as direct dialogue with the Creator, not only liturgical celebrations.

Thirdly, awareness of God's miracles and providence is cultivated by the continual renewal of memory, for example, by observing Sabbath and Passover: "This is why we have so many commandments that remind us of the Exodus so that we always remember God's presence in our lives."[11]

Ramban supports a balanced approach where humans must act responsibly, but always place ultimate trust in God. Unlike Moses Maimonides

9. Nachmanides, *Commentary*, Gen 18:19.
10. Nachmanides, *Commentary*, Exod 13:16.
11. Nachmanides, *Commentary*, Exod 13:16.

(who emphasized faith through philosophical knowledge), Ramban defines faith more relationally. It is not only knowing that God exists, but feeling his nearness. Faith has emotional and personal dimensions, not just intellectual. It requires the engagement of both mind and heart. If everything is a hidden miracle, faith is seeing signs of the divine hand everywhere.

Belief and Trust

We are invited to dwell consciously in God's presence—to see the world not as material or random, but as a divine drama unfolding with purpose. Nachmanides celebrates the life of faith by means of two overlapping, complementary and recurring concepts: *Emunah* (belief) and *Bitachon* (trust).

Emunah, as we noted, fosters a comprehensive awareness that God is present and active in all aspects of life, recognizing God's hand in everything. *Bitachon* is the calm confidence that flows from that awareness: living without fear, because one knows God is in control, trusting that nothing happens by chance. *Bitachon* is an assurance in the depths of our heart and soul that God is watching, caring and holding us. These ideas are both theological and practical, shaping one's view of history, suffering, morality, and personal conduct.

The Rambam defines *Emunah* as the knowledge that God created and continues to run all of creation. Simply put, nothing can exist and no activity can occur without God. We could say that *Emunah* is a state of perspective and outlook shaping our *seeing* while *Bitachon* is a state of trust shaping our *being*. *Emunah* means knowing that God is involved in every activity on the planet; *Bitachon* means discerning and trusting in God in every situation, living with a sense and awareness that everything is under his control, believing that there is no such thing as randomness or chance.

Faith can grow in times of trial, which can turn out to be deeply learning experiences: "He afflicted you and tested you . . . to teach you that man does not live by bread alone . . ."[12] Testing times can bring forth people's potential and teach them trust, discovering that sustenance and success ultimately come from God, not human effort alone. Tests and challenges are meant to build trust in God, not in material means: all our physical needs are met by God's word and will. This ties directly into *Bitachon* : living with trust even in times of scarcity, recognizing that God is the true Provider.

12. Nachmanides, *Commentary,* Deut 8:2.

The practice of fostering a continual God-consciousness or awareness of the Divine leads us to remain calm, kind and spiritually secure, anchoring one's life in humility and cultivating a deep inner security. This is commended in Nachmanides' letter to his son.

NACHMANIDES SPEAKS

When in 1267 Nachmanides moved to Acre in Palestine, he wrote a letter to the son who had remained in Spain. As a tender father, he was concerned that his son would live a godly and upright life, so composed directives to guide him in this moving and motivational letter. Since it was first published three hundred years later, it has become a staple of Jewish ethical literature and is often included in prayer books. In fact, the *Iggeret HaRamban* (Ramban's Letter) is arguably the most well-known and widely published and commonly studied piece of medieval Hebrew literature.

> "Listen, my son, to the thought of your father, and do not forsake the teaching of your mother" (Prov 1:8).
>
> Accustom yourself to always speak all of your words calmly, to every one and at every time. In doing so you will prevent your anger from flaring, which is a bad attribute in people which may cause us to sin. . .
>
> When you will have freed yourself from anger, the quality of humility will enter your heart which is the best of all good traits, as is written (Prov 22:4), "The return for humility is fear of God."
>
> Through humility you will also come to fear God. It will cause you to always think about "where you came from and where you are going," as the Rabbis taught. Remember, you will eventually stand for judgment before the Glorious King, as it is written (1 Kgs 8:27; 2 Chron 6:18) "Even the heaven and the heavens of heaven cannot contain You"; "How much less the hearts of people!" (Prov 15:11). It is also written (Jer 23:24), "'Do I not fill heaven and earth?' says the Lord."
>
> When you think about all these things, you will come to fear God who created you, and you will protect yourself from sinning and thereby be happy with whatever happens to you. Also, when you act humbly and modestly before everyone, and fear God and fear sin, the radiance of His glory and the spirit of the *Shekinah* (Divine Presence) will rest upon you, and you will live the life of the World to Come!

And now, my son, understand and observe that whoever feels that he is greater than others is rebelling against the Kingship of Heaven, because he is adorning himself with His garments, as it is written (Ps 93:1), "The Lord reigns, He wears clothes of pride."

What cause does one have for pride? Perhaps one's wealth? "The Lord impoverishes and enriches" (1 Sam 2:7). Perhaps our honor? It belongs to God, as it is written (1 Chron 29:12), "Wealth and honor come from You." So how could one adorn oneself with God's honor? And one who prides oneself in wisdom surely knows that God "takes away the speech of assured men and reasoning from the sages" (Job 12:20). Thus, all are equal before God, since with His anger He lowers the proud and when He wishes He raises the low. So humble yourself and God will raise you up!

Therefore, I will now explain to you how to always behave humbly. Speak gently at all times, with your head bowed, your eyes looking down to the ground and your heart focusing on God. Don't look at the face of the person to whom you are speaking. Consider everyone as greater than yourself. If they are wise or wealthy, you should give them respect. If they are poor and you are wealthier or wiser than them, consider yourself to be more guilty than them, and that they are more worthy than you, since when they sin it is inadvertent, while you act knowingly!

In all your actions, words and thoughts, always regard yourself as standing before God, with His *Shekinah* above you, for His glory fills the whole world. Speak with fear and awe, as servants in the presence of their master.

Act with restraint in front of everyone. When someone calls you, don't answer loudly, but calmly, as one who stands before their master.

Take heed to study Torah constantly, so you will be able to fulfill its commands. When you arise from your learning reflect carefully on what you have studied, to find a lesson in it that you can put into practice. Examine your actions every morning and evening, and in this way every one of your days will be spent in returning to God.

Remove all worldly concerns from your heart during prayer. Prepare your heart before God, purify your thoughts and think about the words before you utter them.

Do this each and every day of your life, in all of your activities and you will not come to sin. This way all your words, deeds and thoughts will be proper, your prayers will be pure, clear, clean, appropriate and acceptable to God, as it is written (Ps 10:17), "When their heart is directed to You, listen to them."

Read this letter at least once a week and not less. Fulfill it, and in so doing, walk with it forever in the ways of the Lord, may He be blessed, so that you will succeed in all your ways. This is how you will succeed and merit the World to Come which is reserved for the righteous. Every day you read this letter, heaven shall answer whatever arises in your heart to request, forever. Amen, Sela![13]

QUESTIONS FOR REFLECTION

1. What strikes you most about Nachmanides' teaching?
2. How would you express a sense of God's providence? What is your experience of it?
3. How do you understand miracles?
4. What do you make of the Franciscan affirmation: "The purpose of Christ is to work miracles through people who are willing to be emptied of self and to surrender to him. We then become channels of grace through whom his mighty work is done"?[14]
4. Is Nachmanides' teaching any different to St Paul's affirmation "We know that all things work together for good for those who love God, who are called according to his purpose" (Rom 8:28)?
5. What resonances, parallels or contrasts do you see between this chapter's character and Francis of Assisi?

FURTHER READING

Bick, Ezra. " Introduction to the Thought of the Ramban"
etzion.org.il/en/philosophy/great-thinkers/ramban/miracles
Twersky, Isadore. *Rabbi Moses Nachmanides: Explorations in his Religious and Literary Virtuosity.* Cambridge, MA: Harvard University Press, 1983.

13. Nachmanides, *Iggeret HaRamban.*
14. Society of St Francis, Third Order, *Principles,* Day 30.

PART 3

Islamic Luminaries

Arabi

7

Living Imaginatively

Ibn al-Arabi (1165–1240)

OUR ISLAMIC REPRESENTATIVES OF the 12th and 13th centuries are testimonies of the blossoming Sufi tradition, which fostered an intense devotional approach to the Divine, in the face of the predominating—and sometimes distant—sense of God as Absolute Other. These heartwarming writers kindle a flame of desire and love for the Creator, who becomes Lover: transcendence becomes tenderness.

Ibn al-Arabi, often referred to as Shaykh al-Akbar, "the Greatest Master", was a Sufi mystic, philosopher, poet, and theologian whose works have had a profound influence on Islamic spirituality. Idries Shah calls him "One of the most profound metaphysical influences upon both the Muslim and Christian worlds."[1] There is little doubt that he was known to Sultan Malek al-Kamil. Calabria affirms: "Al-Kamil would have been familiar with the Sufi master Ibn al-Arabi, who passed through Egypt at least twice during al-Kamil's lifetime. Ibn al-Arabi is the Sufi most associated with the concept of *al-wahdat al-wajud*, 'the oneness of being.'"[2] His teachings deeply emphasize the inner journey, the spiritual quest of the soul seeking unity with the Divine.

1. Shah, *Sufis*, 166.

2. Calabria, "Introducing the Sultan al-Malik al-Kamil." Franciscan mystic Ramon Llull (1232–1316) was influenced by Ibn al-Arabi.

Ibn al-Arabi was an extraordinary traveler and pilgrim. As a young man in Seville, he studied under mystics, philosophers, and poets. He inhaled the Qur'an, exhaled poetry, and meditated not just in solitude but in cemeteries, caves and marketplaces. One night, aged just fifteen, he secluded himself for retreat. Suddenly, the room was filled with radiant figures: the spirits of the prophets. Jesus, Moses, Muhammad, and others spoke to him in unity, confirming his path. That was the moment, he said, when the veil tore.

His father, on noticing a change in him, mentioned this to philosopher and judge Ibn Rushd (Averroes) who asked to meet Ibn al-Arabi. Ibn al-Arabi said that from this first meeting, he had learned to perceive a distinction between formal knowledge of rational thought and the unveiling of insights into the nature of things. He then adopted Sufism and dedicated his life to the spiritual path.

He ventured as a pilgrim on journeys both physical and inner. His outer itineraries became a mirror of his soul. They manifested his inner restlessness and insatiable quest for the Divine. He wandered across the Islamic world in a quest for knowledge and spiritual enlightenment, involving encounters with numerous teachers, mystical experiences, and the development of his unique philosophical and spiritual system. Ibn al-Arabi's travels were a dramatic spiritual and intellectual journey, marked by significant geographical movement and profound personal transformation. They also represent a certain attitude of spirit: Ibn al-Arabi was prepared to go beyond limits, be they geographical or spiritual.

He left Andalusia for the first time at age 28, journeying to Tunisia, and later Morocco, sojourning at the center of Sufi practice at Fez. As we noted, he passed through Egypt twice during the time of Malek al-Kamil. In 1202 he made his *hajj* to Mecca, a pivotal moment, leading to intense spiritual experiences and the start of his magnum opus *Futuhat al-Makkiyya*, known in English as the *Meccan Illuminations* and becoming a foundational text in Islamic mysticism, destined to influence generations of scholars and practitioners. His travels took him to Konya in Anatolia (1205 and 1210, where Rumi was later to settle), to Mosul in Iraq, Aleppo in Syria and Jerusalem. At every place he encountered Sufi masters and shared his teachings, further solidifying his reputation as a spiritual leader. He eventually settled in Damascus in 1223, where he spent his final years teaching and writing, despite facing criticism from some orthodox scholars.

JOURNEY OF THE HEART

But it was the journey of Mohammed himself which inspired his odyssey of the soul. He recognized in the Prophet's famed mystical night journey from Mecca to the "furthest mosque" *(Al Aqsa)* in Jerusalem an image and archetype of the soul's quest. Moreover he saw in Mohammed's ascension from Jerusalem through the seven heavens to God's throne itself—where he received from God the command of *Salat*, prayer five times a day—a representation of the ascent of the soul to which all are summoned.

According to Ibn al-Arabi, every true seeker is capable of their own inner ascension. The Prophet's physical and spiritual *mi'raj* was unique and perfect, but its pattern is available to every soul. The inner *mi'raj* requires four essentials: purification of the self, remembrance of God (*dhikr*), contemplation and witnessing (*mushahada*).

In the *Meccan Illuminations* he sketches out the levels or steps in the ascent—although described in quasi-spatial terms this is a spiritual journey, a journey of the heart. The inner *mi'raj* (or spiritual ascension) is the soul's journey through the levels of being—from the world of senses and multiplicity to the Divine Presence. It mirrors the Prophet's ascent but happens within the self. While described symbolically as upward in space, the *mi'raj* is inward through consciousness, unveiling higher levels of reality and selfhood. James Winston Morris explains:

> If the journey in question necessarily appears to move through time and distance, that is not so that we can eventually "reach" God—since "He is with you wherever you are"—but rather "so that He can cause [us] to see His Signs" (31:31) that are always there, "on the horizons" and "in the souls." Hence the central importance of the celebrated divine saying (*hadith*) with which he concludes that opening section: "My earth does not encompass Me, nor does My heaven, but the heart of My servant, the one of true faith, does encompass Me."[3]

Two Types of Travelers

Arabi sets two types of traveler side by side, as we shall see in our extract, contrasting two ways of seeking knowledge. On the one hand we find the pilgrim and disciple, characterized by openness of soul, receptive to

3. Morris, "Spiritual Ascension".

intuitive, imaginative insight gained by a risky experiential readiness to welcome whatever is revealed. On the other hand we see the philosopher, committed to logical and rational thinking, the priority of mind over soul. We have seen this contrast before, in the rise of Thomas Aquinas and the Scholastics in the Dominican tradition, and the differences between Moses Maimonides and his son Abraham Maimonides in the Jewish tradition. These days it has been put in popular terms of left/ right brain, though we have been alerted to the advantages of flexible neuroplasticity!

Both approaches are needed, as Arabi points out, but he paints in high relief the respective findings of a teachable disciple and an independent mindset, as they are led on their journey of discovery by the messenger, who can be identified as the Prophet himself or a spiritual guide or mentor. The first leads to encounter, the latter to scientific enquiry. So in the first heaven the philosopher is introduced to interesting aspects of the Moon, while the pilgrim-disciple actually meets Adam. In the second the disciple encounters John the Baptist and Jesus, while the rational thinker is introduced to the mysteries of the planet Mercury. In the third one meets Joseph while the other explores Venus. In the fourth the alternative is between Idis and the Sun, while in the fifth heaven the pilgrim-soul meets Aaron while his companion learns about Mars; it's Moses or Jupiter in the sixth, and Abraham or Saturn in the seventh.

In fact, according to al-Arabi, the rational thinker gets stuck in the seventh heaven, while the disciple continues to progress through the unfolding of divine revelations of the Garden of Paradise and its four rivers, which represent the Qur'an, Torah, Psalms and Gospel, noting "each of them is true, for it is the Word of God."

Next he or she may advance to heavenly mansions and the divine throne. Beyond the supreme Light there is Cloud—representing ultimate majesty and transcendence of the Divine—*Tawhid*, the absolute oneness and unity and mystery of God.

The two travelers return to earth—but by different routes: the thinker retraces his steps but the pilgrim experiences a different way. This expresses the idea that he or she is transformed, and will never be the same again.[4] The two travelers do meet up again to share their experiences. The thinker resolves to undertake the journey again, but as an open-hearted pilgrim next time!

4. Arabi develops this through the idea of alchemy—processes by which iron and base metals are turned to gold.

Islamic scholar William Chittick notes:

> In another account of the ascent to God, Ibn al-Arabi tells the story in the first person. Here he suggests that achieving perfection demands realizing the Real in the full expanse of His self-disclosure within one's very *wujud*, one's existence/finding [our inner essential being]. After describing the stages of his own climb in Muhammad's footsteps, he concludes:
>
> "In this journey I gained the meanings of all the divine names. I saw that they all go back to One Named Object, One Entity. That Named Object was what I was witnessing, and that [divine] Entity was my own *wujud* [my very being]. So, my journey had been only in myself. I have provided no indications of anything but myself."
>
> This last sentence can stand for the entire contents of *The Meccan Illuminations*, Ibn al-Arabi's grand catalogue of the doorways to the Real: "I have provided no indications of anything but myself." The self in question is the human essence, created in the image of God and receptive to every name taught by the Divine Teacher. Recognizing this self—to whatever extent one is able to do so—brings forth intimations of the life of the heart. Such recognition will never be found by blindly imitating jurists and theologians, not to speak of the thinkers and dreamers of our own times. It will only come by patient knocking at the door.[5]

A *hadith* often attributed to the Prophet "He who knows himself knows his Lord"—this might sum up the teaching of Ibn al-Arabi.

Perceiving Imaginatively

In part Ibn al-Arabi's vision of the mystical ascent to God through the seven heavens comes from his inspired imaginative thinking. Ibn al-Arabi placed imagination (*khayal*) at the very center of his metaphysical system. For him, imagination was not merely fantasy or subjective daydreaming but an ontological reality, a mode of being and perceiving that connects the Divine and the human.

Ibn al-Arabi begins with the idea of the creative imagination as a reflection of God's own act of creation. As in Genesis 1 the world comes into existence by God's uttered Word (Heb. *Dabar*)—"He spoke and it came to be", developed in John's Gospel's "In the beginning was the Word" (Gr.

5. Chittick, "Doorway to an Intellectual Tradition".

Logos), so for Ibn al-Arabi the world is God's dream, his vision: God "imagined" the cosmos into existence ("Be! and it is"). As characters in God's dream, humans mirror this divine creativity through imagination: which is thus a participation in divine creativity, not an illusion.

Spiritual knowledge, prophecy and vision come through our God-given capacity for imagination, a sort of faculty for contemplating the Divine. Imagination is a *barzakh* (isthmus or bridge)—a threshold between the spiritual and material. It is a vehicle or means of God's revelation to humans. It is true, ordinary imagination may produce illusions, but purified imagination becomes a mirror of divine truth, and a means of perception, by which we come to glimpse the Divine through symbols and images. As we learn to live imaginatively, ever alert to God in every way, we move in the flow of divine creativity. Imagination opens the door to a type of experiential or mystical knowledge that purely rational thought cannot reach. To live imaginatively is to live intuitively, ever open to new perceptions or intimations of the Divine. As Halligan puts it:

> Ibn al-Arabi views the Active Imagination as both a conscious—willed—and spontaneous, autonomous process. Through surrender and annihilation in the Divine, the mystic opens himself to receive theophanies, resulting in a life lived perpetually in awareness of Divine Presence. Union with the Divine is the aim of the mystic and Ibn al-Arabi shows us a detailed account of how that life is experienced.[6]

Akkach concours:

> In Ibn al-Arabi's ontology imagination plays an essential role: it is seen as the creative source of manifestation, the very cause of our existence, and the powerful intermediary that enables us to remain in constant contact with the Infinite and the Absolute. Through the concept of imagination Ibn al-Arabi managed to differentiate between the human and Divine mechanism of creativity, a differentiation which he then used to resolve the paradox of the eternity (*qidam*) and newness (*hudūth*) of the world.[7]

6. Halligan, "Creative Imagination of the Sufi Mystic, Ibn Arabi."
7. Akkach, "World of Imagination in Ibn Arabi's Ontology", 98.

Seeing the World as Theophany

As Ibn al-Arabi trains himself to discern the Divine in the world, he realizes that we are called to live contemplatively—contemplation takes place not just on the prayer mat, but in the midst of daily life. We start to see every human face as reflecting something of the divine countenance, and to honor every human life as a sacred locus of theophany, a place where God speaks to us and reveals Godself to us. Each moment becomes a unique epiphany of the Real, an occasion for the self-disclosure of God.

Ibn al-Arabi's outlook is underpinned by his vision of *al-wahdat al-wajud*, the oneness of being. He sees past the multiplicity of things in a fragmented world to its underlying unity in God. This isn't exactly pantheism but a vision of the universe where God is the only true Reality: God not an external being acting on the world but the world itself. Some found Ibn al-Arabi's teaching controversial, but this doctrine is not just abstract philosophy: it shapes spiritual vision and one's way of living and reacting. We're invited to perceive every creature, every event, as a theophany—a manifestation of Divine Names: to see God in all things is to realize *wahdat al-wujud* in lived experience:

> To practice imagination is to honor the truth that comes through your own dreams, your moments of creative insight, and your deepest intuitions. It is to learn to read the symbolic language of your own soul, understanding that this is a primary medium through which the Divine communicates.[8]

IBN AL-ARABI SPEAKS

> [The guide asks: "What do you seek?"]
>
> The two travelers replied: "We seek knowledge of the One who has appointed us as *khalifa* [guardians] over our corporeal body."
>
> [The guide] says: "God has made me a messenger to my own kind, to clarify for them the way of knowledge which leads to Him, wherein lies their true happiness."
>
> Then one of them replies: "That is exactly what I have been looking for. So do teach me knowledge of this path that I may follow it."

8. Sapienta Mundi, *Wisdom of Ibn Arabi*, 84.

However, the other says: "I would like to discover the path of knowing Him by myself. I do not just want to follow you unconditionally in it. Why should I be so lacking in aspiration as to simply imitate you?" So this person will not heed his words, but he starts to think and theorize about that question with his intellect... Such is the position of one who obtains their knowledge through intellectual proofs by rational thought.

The former, on the other hand, typifies those who consciously follow the messenger and those who unquestioningly accept him with regard to what he explains about the knowledge of their Maker...

So the two men—or rather two individuals, as it might be two women or one woman and one man—follow the path, one by virtue of using rational thought and the other by virtue of being a disciple.

They both begin to engage in spiritual training, which is the refining of character; spiritual endeavor, which is enduring bodily hardship like hunger; and devotional acts such as standing in prayer a long time and persevering tirelessly in it, fasting, going on pilgrimage, spiritual warfare and wandering. The one does this using his own rational intelligence, and the other through what is prescribed for him by his teacher and instructor . . .

When the door of the nearest heaven is opened to them, the disciple meets Adam, who is delighted with him and seats him by his side. Meanwhile, the one who relies upon his own reason meets the spiritual entity of the moon, which seats him at its side.

As the guest of the moon, the rational thinker sees all the knowledge it possesses: how it cannot go beyond the elemental spheres which lie below it, how it has no knowledge of what lies above it. . .At the same time he realizes how Adam possesses the knowledge of places beneath him and above him, and how he extends to *his* guest from what he has, which is not within the capacity of the moon to be aware of. He knows that Adam only reveals it to him as a blessing and grace from the instructor, who is the messenger. . .

The disciple, who is Adam's guest, is taught by his father as much about the divine Names as Adam sees that his temperament can bear. Individual souls are not all at the same level of receptivity: one can receive what others do not. In the first of the heavens, he learns from Adam's knowledge by way of the private divine face [direct personal relationship with God]. The rational thinker has no knowledge of this face at all. The knowledge of the private face is the science of the elixir of the mystics. (I too would not have mentioned it were it not for the fact that I have been commanded to give counsel to this community, indeed to all the servants of God.)

The rational thinker, who is the guest of the moon only comes to know about the physical effects and transformations that take place in the bodily substances composed of natural elements. The disciple on the other hand, receives what this celestial sphere specifically contains in terms of divine Knowledge, which individual souls may obtain, how that relates to the Being of the Real. . .

Everything that the rational thinker acquires is also acquired by the disciple, but not everything that the disciple obtains is obtained by the rational thinker. The rational thinker cannot grow and develop except in sadness and distress, and they cannot confirm the truth until their journey comes to an end and they return to their body. . .The disciple sees constant progress which accompanies him wherever he goes, because it comes from the private face, which is recognized only by the one who possesses it.

When they have both stayed in this heaven as long as God wishes, they set off again on the journey, bidding farewell to their respective hosts. They rise in their spiritual ascension to the second heaven. . .[9]

QUESTIONS FOR REFLECTION

1. What kind of things, do you think, are discoverable by intuition and not by logic? How do you respond to the saying: "He who knows himself knows his Lord"? How can self-knowledge become a way of discovering God?
2. In our reading, the pilgrim is characterized by a certain vulnerability, while self control, even barriers, mark out the rational thinker. Both share curiosity and spiritual thirst. What is your default mode?
3. Do you need a spiritual guide or mentor? Is God calling you to be a spiritual guide or supporter to someone in their spiritual journey?
4. What do you make of Ibn al-Arabi's words: "Individual souls are not all at the same level of receptivity: one can receive what others do not"? How, do you think, is it possible to develop an intuition or awareness of the Divine, as the pilgrim experienced?

9. Ibn al-Arabi, *Alchemy of Human Happiness*, 69–76.

5. What resonances, parallels or contrasts do you see between this chapter's character and Francis of Assisi?
6. How do you find yourself responding to Arabi's words:

> My heart has become capable of every form:
> it is a pasture for gazelles and a convent for Christian monks,
> and a temple for idols and the pilgrim's Ka'bah
> and the tables of the Torah and the book of the Qur'an.
> I follow the religion of Love: whatever way Love's camels take,
> that is my religion and my faith.[10]

FURTHER READING

Austin, Ralph W. J., trans. *Ibn Al-Arabi: The Bezels of Wisdom*. New York: Paulist, 1980.

Chittick, William. *The Sufi Path of Knowledge: Ibn Al-Arabi's Metaphysics of Imagination*. New York: State University of New York Press, 1989.

Cutsinger, James S., ed. *Paths to the Heart: Sufism and the Christian East*. Bloomington, Indiana: World Wisdom, 2002.

Drayson, Elizabeth. *Crucible of Light: Islam and the forging of Europe from the 8th to the 21st Century*. Basingstoke: Picador, 2025.

10. Al-Arabi, *Tarjuman al-ashwaq*, Ghazal 11.

Farid

8

Living Passionately

Ibn al-Farid (1181–1235)

IBN AL-FARID WAS A celebrated Sufi poet of the 12th–13th century, often called *"the Sultan of Lovers"* (*Sultan al-Ashiqin*). Regarded as one of the greatest mystical poets in Arabic literature, he is famous for his profound expressions of divine love, unity with God, and mystical intoxication.

It is highly likely that the name of Ibn al-Farid came up frequently during the conversations at Damietta between Francis and Malek al-Kamil, for the Sultan was a great admirer of his poetry and they may well have met in person. The Sultan patronized the arts and sciences, and his study sessions with scholars were well known. Ibn al-Farid's grandson Ali, in an account of his grandfather's life, tells us that on one occasion the Sultan's secretary Sharaf al-Din recited before him a beautiful poem. When he was told that this was a composition by Ibn al-Farid, the Sultan commanded his secretary:

> Take one thousand of our dinars and go to him and say on my behalf, "Your son Muhammad greets you and requests that you accept this from him in the name of the mendicants who come to you." If he accepts it, ask him to attend us that we may take our share of his spiritual blessings *[barakah]*.[1]

1. Ibn al- Farid's grandson, Ali (1334), who contributed most to the poet's recognition as a holy man. Ali made a collection of his grandfather's poetry, prefaced by an account of Ibn al-Farid's adult life. Naqshbandi Haqqani Rabbani, "Umar-Ibn-al-Farid."

Malek was inspired by his stunning verse, which communicated powerfully the Sufi discovery of the Divine. Ibn al-Farid declined the money, choosing to trust in God to supply for his needs. He did not want to be drawn into the mold of a well-paid court-poet, like some of his contemporaries, but to be free to write and teach without obligations. His position as a teacher at the Al-Azhar Mosque in Cairo allowed him to provide for his family, which included three children.

Born in Cairo into a family of jurists, he had been expected to study Islamic law. His Syrian-born father was a respected *farid,* an advocate for women's causes. Yet, from an early age, he rejected the path of judgeship and legal disputes. Instead, he wandered the hills of Cairo, seeking solitude and prayer. His refusal of a safe career was his first rebellion, a startling move for a young man of his class.

As a young man Ibn al-Farid went on extended spiritual retreats among the oases, specifically the Oasis of the Wretches (Wadi al-Mustad'afin), outside Cairo. In search of greater progress he enrolled in a *madrasa* (theological college). But his life was turned around by a "chance" encounter with a shopkeeper performing the ritual Muslim ablutions outside the door of the *madrasa*. The grocer looked at him and said, "Umar! You will not be enlightened in Egypt. You will be enlightened only in Mecca."

Umar Ibn al-Farid was stunned by this statement, sensing that this simple greengrocer was no ordinary man. When he argued that he couldn't possibly make the trip to Mecca right away, the man gave Ibn al-Farid a vision, in that very moment, of Mecca. Ibn al-Farid was so transfixed by this experience that he left immediately for the holy city and, in his own words, "Then as I entered it, enlightenment came to me wave after wave and never left".

Umar Ibn al-Farid stayed in Mecca for fifteen years, engaged in mystic studies and immersing himself in the practices of pilgrimage. He also composed much of his poetry, renowned for its mystical themes, during his time in Mecca. While in Mecca, he became a Shaykh, plunging himself into a disciplined Sufi life, marked by study, fasting, prayer and meditations sometimes leading to an ecstatic state.

Eventually he returned to Cairo because he heard the same greengrocer calling him back to attend his funeral. Upon his return he found the grocer on the point of death, and they wished each other farewell.

Upon al-Farid's return to Cairo, he was treated as a saint. He would hold teaching sessions with judges, viziers and other leaders of the city. While walking down the street, people would come up to him and crowd around him, seeking spiritual blessings (*barakah*) and try to kiss his hand (he would respond by shaking their hand). Ibn al-Farid thrived as a scholar of Muslim law, a teacher of the *hadith* and a teacher of poetry. Eyewitnesses said he looked like a man intoxicated, staggering through Cairo's streets in ecstatic states. His appearance shocked respectable society, but Sufis recognized the mark of mystical rapture. He lived between scandal and sainthood, condemned by the orthodox but adored by mystics.

Sometime later the Sultan was informed that Ibn al-Farid had returned to Cairo, but in poor health. The Sultan sent one of his amirs to ask Ibn al-Farid's permission to build a tomb for him under al-Shafid's dome and next to the grave of the sultan's mother. But Ibn al-Farid denied this request and another, which proposed the construction of a shrine especially for him. In these stories al-Malek al-Kamil is clearly portrayed as an admirer of both Ibn al-Farid's poetry and holiness, and he hoped to win the poet's favor and spiritual blessings through patronage.

Ibn al-Farid died in Cairo in 1235, reportedly in a state of mystical ecstasy. After his death, legends spread that his grave exuded light and fragrance. Some claimed to have seen him in visions guiding them on the path. Revered by Sufis for his spiritual depth and by literary scholars for his mastery of Arabic poetic form, his works influenced later Sufi poets, including Rumi.

His shrine in Cairo became (and still is) a place of pilgrimage for lovers of poetry and seekers of divine love.

FOUR THEMES

1 The Spiritual Journey

His greatest work is *The Mystic Way* (*al-Ta'iyya al-Kubra*). It is not systematized but seven overlapping themes are celebrated, offering if not a roadmap then a sketch of the mystic's path:

Awakening An inner restlessness indicates that the soul is yearning for a deeper experience of God. A spark of love awakens, the call of the Beloved. Ibn al-Farid portrays this as hearing a distant voice of the Divine, pulling him away from worldly illusions.

Detachment Seekers begin to let go of their grasp of material attachments and ego-driven desires. This is not so much about rejecting the world, but about seeing it differently: as a veil covering divine reality. The lover chooses poverty (*faqr*) in God over wealth in the world.

Struggles The ego (*nafs*) resists surrender. Tests of patience, trust, and surrender follow. The lover feels lost, wounded, intoxicated; this suffering is a hidden mercy leading to transformation. The seeker experiences both the sweetness and pain of love: longing when apart, ecstasy when near.

Ego-Annihilation The seeker begins to dissolve in God's presence as personal identity, pride, and will fade away. Ibn al-Farid often uses metaphors of wine and intoxication here: being drunk on God's love until nothing of the self remains.

Union with the Beloved The climax of the path: the lover and Beloved are no longer two, duality and separation are overcome. He describes becoming a mirror in which God beholds Himself. The lines blur: is he the lover speaking, or God through him?

Living faithfully in God After annihilation comes permanence. The seeker returns to daily life, but now it is God's light shining through him. This is not escape from the world, but living in it with a transformed vision.

Return to Humanity The knower comes back to live among people with humility. Outwardly, one is ordinary; inwardly, one is in constant union. Our task now is service, compassion, and guiding others.

2 Spiritual Intoxication

His poem *The Wine Ode (al-Khamriyah)* describes a "wine older than the vine," a wine that brings clarity, not drunkenness. It uses the metaphor of wine to symbolize the divine love and inebriation discovered in the soul's journey. The wine, in this context, can be seen as a representation of the divine essence, and the lover's longing for it is a metaphor for the Sufi's yearning for union with God.

Paul Smith puts it:

> The subject of the *Wine Poem* and the *Mystic's Progress* is this Divine Love (wine) for which the Beloved feels for the lover and which the lover longs for, and experiences flowing from the Beloved's cup (heart) to him, filling his heart (cup) to overflowing. If the lover cannot feel this flow of love from God, this causes him great pain and despair.
>
> By using such sensuous imagery Ibn al-Farid spiritualizes the physical and uses a language understandable to all. . .Through such imagery he expresses the agony and ecstasy of his direct experience of God and makes these experiences available for all to share. . .[2]

2. Smith, *Diwan of Ibn Al-Farid*, 29.

This language was considered risqué.[3] Many jurists accused him of heresy, thinking he praised forbidden wine and finding the language outrageous and scandalous. This misunderstanding gave him both fame and notoriety: he was celebrated by mystics, but condemned by literalists.

> But they said, "You've drunk sin!"
> No, indeed, I drank only
> that whose abstention
> is in to me. . .
> While it made me drunk
> before my birth,
> abiding always with me
> though my bones be worn away.
> So take it straight,
> though if you must, then mix it,
> but your turning away
> from the beloved's mouth is wrong. . .
> For there is no life in this world
> for one who lives here sober;
> who does not die drunk on it,
> prudence has passed him by.[4]

3 Intimacy with the Divine

> Ancient is my tale of love for her;
> it has, she knows, no beginning, no end,
> and there is none like me in passion for her,
> while her enchanting beauty has no equal! . . .
> Whether in parting's anger or passion's acceptance,
> you are with me, my heart holding you every hour.
> He was a lion taming the lions of the jungle
> until he fell victim to a young gazelle.
> So it happened that passion's fire filled him;
> he sees its burning but no relief.[5]

These lines convey something of the passionate love Farid has for his Creator. The often erotic language of intimacy communicates the intensity of desire for God as for a lover who has captivated one's heart. But this yearning

3. Early Church fathers such as Gregory of Nyssa and Ambrose of Milan also wrote of "sober intoxication" or "spiritual inebriation" to describe joyful union with God.

4. Homerin, *Sufi Verse, Saintly Life*, 50,51.

5. Homerin, *Passion Before Me*, 35,36, 44.

after God's beauty and craving for the bliss of union is tempered by various degrees of suffering: the pain of separation and the sense of being wounded by divine Love, a desired annihilation of the ego (*fana*)—the heart emptied of selfishness to be filled with the Beloved. Farid evokes images of the popular Sufi exercise of *dhikr,* "recollection" or meditation on the presence of God within oneself, a practice supported by the divine saying: "My heavens and earth do not embrace Me, but the heart of My faithful servant does embrace." *Dhikr* is the characteristic Sufi spiritual discipline: the corporate recital or chanting of the 99 divine names accompanied by rhythmic swaying of the body, participants sitting or standing within a circle.

Ibn al-Farid's poetry frequently uses feminine imagery and symbolism to express the relationship between the soul and the Divine. Celebrating the concepts of beauty, grace, and the Beloved, this feminine language highlights the intimate and relational aspects of Sufi spirituality. The "Beloved" in his *Mystic Way* is called "She" or "Her" and depicted with feminine qualities, reflecting a mystical experience where the Divine is not solely viewed as transcendent and masculine, but also immanent and feminine. As we will notice elsewhere, Sufi thought, including Ibn al-Farid's, often incorporates the concept of the "Divine Feminine," not as a separate deity, but as an aspect of God's attributes manifested in the world. This feminine aspect is seen as a source of compassion, contributing to the Sufi understanding of God's multifaceted nature. In Sufism, while feminine imagery is used, it never entails a literal or exclusive association of the Divine with the feminine. Rather it prompts the call to transcend gendered categories as we seek a state of spiritual unity and oneness with the Divine.

4 Everyday Mysticism

Ibn Al-Farid's time in Mecca, living in the environs of the Ka'ba was hugely formative, and of course stayed with him for the rest of his life. His heart was always in Mecca:

> My heart has inclined to the holy sanctuary,
> and even if my body dwells elsewhere,
> it never departs from Mecca.
> Its longing circles the Ka'ba,
> as the pilgrims circle it in devotion.

In Sufi interpretation, Mecca here is not only the sacred city: it's also the inner Ka'ba of the heart, the place where divine love dwells. That's why he says even if he is far away, his spirit is always present there. As we shall see powerfully expressed in our extract, al-Farid celebrates the sanctification of every time and place. While ever treasuring memories of Mecca, he returns to bustling, commercial Cairo and finds the sacred unveiled everywhere. The concept of "holy places" becomes expanded beyond shrines to embrace the homes and streets and market places of every neighborhood. Similarly, all time can be sacred time. Every day can feel like a holy Friday, dedicated to prayers. Every season can enjoy the blessings of festival days. In Christian terms, we would say it can be Christmas and Easter everyday!

IBN AL-FARID SPEAKS

If she [my Beloved] unveiled
on a holy day,
every tribe would flock to gaze
on her loveliness.
For their spirits long
for her deep beauty,
and in her loveliness,
their eyes find a garden.
Every day is my holy day
when I see
with an eye refreshed
the beauty of her face;
Every night is the Night of Power [when Qur'an given to Mohammed]
when she draws near,
and every day we meet
is one of union, holy Friday.
My running to her [as in Hajj ritual]
is a pilgrimage;
every standing at her door,
the Standing [as at Mount Arafat].
And so wherever she alights
among God's many lands,
though it cool my eye,
I see it not, but Mecca.

Any place that holds her
is a precinct holy;
every house where she resides
is Medina.
Wherever she dwells
is Jerusalem, most sacred
whose soothing sight
cools my burning heart.
And my Farthest Mosque [Al Aksa]
is where she trails her robe;
my musk, the moist earth
where she walked.
The dwellings of my joy,
the tower of my desire,
the limits of my longings,
and refuge from my fear,
were abodes where fate
never entered between us,
nor did shifty time
ensnare us with separation.
The days did not seek
to scatter our union,
nor did the nights
judge between us cruelly. . .
No time was favored
over another in pleasure:
with her, all my moments
are sweet seasons.
My whole day is vesper time
if its first hours
spread her fragrant reply
to my greetings,
And my whole night there
is an enchanting dawn
if a sweet-scented breeze
arises from her to me.
For if she comes at night,
my month by her becomes
the Night of Power, radiant,
as she visits me.
And if she draws near my home,
my year becomes
the spring season
luxuriant amid meadows.

For if she is pleased with me
my whole life will be
the pleasant time of childhood
and the age of youth.
For my heart has drawn together
all love and pain for her,
revealing to you
every desire. . .
Every atom of me
witnessing her loveliness
with every glance
of every shing eye. . .
Every bit of me
hearing her word
with the ear
of all hoping to hear.
Every part of me
kissing her veil
with every mouth
in each touching kiss. . .
What I found so beautiful in her,
bestowed on me by enlightenment,
was an unveiling
driving out every doubt.[6]

QUESTIONS FOR REFLECTION

1. What is your experience of finding God in "holy places"? What is a "holy place" to you? How can we hone our physical and spiritual senses to be alert and responsive to the Divine in the everyday?
2. Where might you locate yourself on Farid's map or sketch of the spiritual journey?
3. How comfortable are you with the language of spiritual intimacy and intoxication?
4. Ibn al-Farid images the Divine in feminine terms, while in the Christian tradition (for example "Bridal Mysticism") the soul is seen as a feminine lover/bride and the Beloved/Bridegroom is Christ. How do you find yourself responding to what is called "the Divine Feminine"?

6. Homerin, *Sufi Verse, Saintly Life*, 175–83.

5. What resonances, parallels or contrasts do you see between this chapter's character and Francis of Assisi?

FURTHER READING

Chittick, William C. *Sufism*. Oxford: One World, 2000.

Douglas-Klotz, Neil. *Sufi Book of Life: 99 Pathways of the Heart for the Modern Dervish*. NY: Berkley, 2005.

Nasr, Seyyed Hossein. *Islamic Spirituality: Manifestations*. London: SCM, 1991.

Nicholson, Reynold A. *The Mystics of Islam*. Beirut: Khayats, 1966.

Derin, Suleyman. *Love in Sufism: From Rabia to Ibn al-Farid*. Istanbul: Insan Yayınları, 2008.

Rumi by Hossein Behzad (1957)

9

Living Daringly

Rumi (1207–1273) and Rabia (710–801)

RABIA—PRECURSOR TO RUMI

Before we turn to Francis' contemporary Rumi, we first pay tribute to an astonishing woman who can rightly be hailed as his precursor, Rabia—she stands before us in her own right. Way back in the eighth century Rabia laid the groundwork for the spiritual ideals and devotional practices that characterized later Sufis like Rumi. Her life and teachings, particularly her articulation of divine love, provided a powerful example and philosophical underpinning for the devotional path that Rumi and others explored in their spiritual journeys and poetry. Rabia al-Adawiyya was a pioneering figure in Sufism, known for her concept of love as a selfless, unconditional devotion to God, not motivated by fear of hell or desire for paradise.

Sufi writers such as Farid al-Din Attar (1145—1221), a major influence on Rumi, highlighted Rabia's importance, acknowledging her spiritual authority and influence on the male mystics who came after her. Indeed Attar provides us with a link in the chain. Attar met Rumi as a young man in 1216 in Nishapur (near the north east border of present Iran). Rumi famously stated, "Attar traveled all seven cities of love, while I'm still at the bend of its first valley."[1] Attar gave him a copy of his *Lives of the Saints, Tadhkirat al-Awliya.* As Gooch affirms: "In his *Lives of the Saints* Attar told

1. Wolpé, *Conference of the Birds,* 5.

of Rabia, the woman mystic of Basra... these stories were lore the boy Rumi either already knew or was now discovering."[2] Attar had written of Rabia:

> That one set apart in the seclusion of holiness, that woman veiled with the veil of religious sincerity, that one on fire with love and longing, that one enamored of the desire to approach her Lord and be consumed in His glory, that woman who lost herself in union with the Divine, that one accepted by men as a second spotless Mary—Rabia al-Adawiyya, may God have mercy upon her. If anyone were to say, "Why have you made mention of her in the class of men?", I should say... if it is allowable to accept two thirds of our faith from Aisha the trustworthy, [Muhammad's highly respected youngest wife] it is also allowable to accept religious benefit from one of her handmaids, Rabia.[3]

Daniel Ladinsky observes: "Rabia is without doubt the most popular and influential of female Islamic saints and a central figure in the Sufi tradition. Although it is rarely said, she, perhaps more than any other poet, influenced Rumi's writings."[4] Both Rabia and Rumi explored the idea of loving God for God's own sake, without the need for external rewards or punishments. Rumi's poetry frequently uses imagery and language that echoes Rabia's emphasis on selfless love and the yearning for union with the Divine.

The great female Sufi mystic, whose tomb stands next to the Mosque of the Ascension atop the Mount of Olives, was born in the Iraqi city of Basra in 710. She had crossed the deserts to reach Jerusalem. A Sufi poet, singer, and mystic, Rabia pioneered the daring use of the language of intimacy for the Divine, famously developed by Rumi. God was for her the only Beloved—stunningly beautiful herself and frequently pursued by would-be lovers, she consecrated herself body and soul to God. She had been enslaved until the man who purchased her saw light radiating around her one evening while she was kneeling in prayer. Rabia went on to compose lyrical love poems describing her unquenchable love for God, and many writings became attributed to her. Camille Adams Helminski explains her significance:

> As the mystical side of Islam developed, it was a woman who first expressed the relationship with the Divine in a language we have come to recognize as specifically Sufic by referring to God as the Beloved. Rabia was the first human being to speak of the realities

2. Gooch, *Rumi's Secret*, 56.
3. Attar, *Memorial of God's Friends [Lives of the Saints]*, 34.
4. Ladinsky, *Poems From God*, 1.

> of Sufism with a language that anyone could understand. Though she experienced many difficulties in her early years, Rabia's starting point was neither a fear of hell nor a desire for paradise, but only love. "God is God", she said—for this I love God . . . not because of any gifts, but for itself—her aim was to melt her being in God. According to her, one could find God by turning within oneself.[5]

Rabia lived life on the edge—even on the brink of eternity. She was a person of great courage and daring. She was known for daring feats of spiritual devotion, such as walking to Mecca with an emaciated donkey that came back to life after she prayed for it, refusing marriage and worldly possessions, and living an independent ascetic life that defied traditional gender roles. She is revered as the first female Sufi saint, celebrated for her unwavering love and devotion to God, and her teachings on divine love

Rabia demonstrated courage through her radical devotion to God, rejecting worldly desires and fears of punishment or reward, and challenging societal norms by living a life of extreme poverty and spiritual independence as a renowned Sufi mystic and one of Islam's earliest female saints. Rabia refused normal ambitions of marriage and wealth because she asserted that her heart was so filled with love for God that there was no room for anyone or anything else.

She challenged the traditional Sufi focus on avoidance of hell or achievement of heaven: "I want to put out the fires of Hell and burn Paradise so that both veils may disappear and no one may worship God for fear of Hell or desire for Paradise, but only for the sake of His eternal beauty."[6]

Despite being a woman in a male-dominated society, Rabia commanded respect from prominent scholars and Sufi masters, who sought her spiritual counsel. With her independent spirit, Rabia was unafraid to assert herself and directly rebuke men who approached her with amorous attention and intentions, reminding them of their distractions from God.

Rabia's courageous spirit and pure devotion left a lasting impact on Sufism, establishing a path of radical love for God that resonated across centuries and continues to illuminate spiritual seekers. She is celebrated as a pioneer, challenging barriers of gender and barriers of language. It is her courage in pushing forward the use of daring language and in expanding a vocabulary of prayer and adoration that is perhaps her greatest legacy and inspiration to Rumi.

5. Helminski, *Women of Sufism,* 23.

6. Attar, *Memorial of God's Friends,* [*Lives of the Saints*], 44.

RABIA SPEAKS

Let's listen to her voice singing across the centuries:

> O God, the stars are shining;
> All eyes have closed in sleep:
> The kings have locked their doors.
> Each lover is alone, in secret, with the one he loves.
> And I am here too: hidden from all of them –
> With You[7]
>
> How long will you keep pounding an open door
> Begging for someone to open it?[8]
>
> . . .lift the veil
> And let me feast my eyes on Your Living Face[9]
>
> In love, nothing exists between breast and Breast.
> Speech is born out of longing.
> True description from the real taste.
> The one who tastes, knows;
> The one who explains, lies.[10]
>
> O God,
> Whenever I listen to the voice of anything You have made –
> The rustling of the trees
> The trickling of water
> The cries of birds
> The flickering of shadow
> The roar of the wind
> The song of the thunder,.
> I hear it saying:
>
> God is One!
> Nothing can be compared with God![11]

Rabia composes a new list of divine names:

7. Upton, *Doorkeeper of the Heart*, 66.
8. Upton, *Doorkeeper of the Heart*, 63.
9. Upton, *Doorkeeper of the Heart*, 6.
10. Upton, *Doorkeeper of the Heart*, 31.
11. Upton, *Doorkeeper of the Heart*, 58.

My Joy
My Hunger
My Shelter
My Friend
My Food for the Journey
My Journey's End
You are my breath,
My hope,
My companion,
My craving,
My abundant wealth. . .
My Life, my Love. . .
O Captain of my Heart,
Radiant Eye of Yearning in my breast. . .
Be satisfied with me, Love
And I am satisfied.[12]

Referring to the practice of the Remembrance of God she writes:

Your hope in my heart is the rarest treasure
Your Name on my tongue is the sweetest word
My choicest hours
Are the hours I spend with You-

O God, I can't live in this world
Without remembering You –[13]

Give the goods of this world to Your enemies –
Give the treasures of Paradise to Your friends –
But as for me—You are all I need.

O God!
If I adore You out of fear of Hell, burn me in Hell!
If I adore You out of desire for Paradise,
Lock me out of Paradise.
But if I adore You for Yourself alone,
Do not deny to me Your eternal beauty.[14]

12. Upton, *Doorkeeper of the Heart*, 57.
13. Upton, *Doorkeeper of the Heart*, 51.
14. Upton, *Doorkeeper of the Heart*, 47.

RUMI

Jalaluddin Rumi, the most appreciated Sufi poet in the West and known to the first generations of Franciscans, was born in Balkh, in present-day Afghanistan. Fleeing the Tartar invasions under the command of the Mongol tyrant Genghis Khan, he traveled with his family as a refugee and migrant through Nishapur (now Iran, where he met Attar), Baghdad, Mecca, Medina, Aleppo, meeting Franciscans, and Damascus, where he met Ibn al-Arabi. Ibn al-Arabi, seeing Rumi walk behind his father, exclaimed: "Glory be to God! An ocean is walking behind a lake!"[15] Finally he settled in Konya (present-day Turkey) in the 1220s. He pursued further studies in Damascus (1230s–1240s). "The map of Rumi's life stretches over 2,500 miles," says Brad Gooch.[16] In 1244, Rumi met in Konya Shams of Tabriz, a wandering dervish traveling across the Islamic world in search of a true spiritual companion. Their intense and extraordinary relationship became a turning point, transforming Rumi from a respected jurist and scholar into one of the greatest mystical poets of all time. Rumi remained in Konya until his death in 1273.

Pioneer of the Spirit

Coleman Barks, who has made new translations from the Persian, celebrates: "His startling imaginative freshness. The deep longing that we feel coming through. His sense of humor. There's always a playfulness mixed in with the wisdom."[17] Jawid Mojaddedi, a scholar of early and medieval Sufism at Rutgers University and an award-winning Rumi translator observes:

> Rumi was an experimental innovator among the Persian poets. . .
>
> The first of Rumi's four main innovations is his direct address to readers in the rare second person. Contemporary readers respond well to this directness.
>
> Second is his urge to teach: Readers of "inspirational" literature are drawn to Rumi's poetry.
>
> Third, his use of everyday imagery.
>
> And fourth, his optimism of the attainment of union within his lyrical love ghazals [odes]. The convention in that form is to

15. Harvey, *Way of Passion*, 64.
16. Gooch, *Rumi's Secret*, 5.
17. Ciabattari, "Why is Rumi the best-selling poet in the US?"

> stress its unattainability and the cruel rebuffs of the beloved. Rumi celebrates union.[18]

Of course, we might add that Rumi also planted the seeds for the development of the role of dance and the body in prayer. After his death, the Mevlevi order, encouraged the spiritual practice of spinning movements connected with meditation and repetition of the divine names, later associated with the "whirling dervishes".

Rumi popularized the Sufi tradition, originating with Rabia, of calling prayer "a path of love", where the Sufi becomes the "lover" and God the "Beloved." This love affair seeks ultimate union with the Beloved. This love relationship is depicted in most volumes of Sufi literature and poetry, but Rumi gives clearest expression to it through his sensuous language:

> Strip off the veil and speak out, for do not I
> enter under the same coverlet as the Beloved?.[19]

He describes the true Sufi in these terms:

> What makes the Sufi? Purity of heart;
> not the patched mantle. . .
> He in all dregs discerns the essence pure:
> in hardship ease, in tribulation joy.
>
> We are the flute, our music is all Yours;
> We are the mountains echoing only You
> and move to defeat or victory;
> Lions emblazoned high on flags unfurled –
> Your wind invisible sweeps us through the world.[20]

Out of the pain of separation from his beloved Shams emerges the theme of taking courage, being ready to embrace suffering and present challenges and future possibilities. Rumi exhorts: "Heart be brave, just go. Love's glory is not a small thing." Rumi's writings encourage courage as an inner quality to face life's challenges, urging individuals to be resolute, take risks, and trust their inner wisdom over fear and the status quo. He suggests that true courage involves embracing vulnerability, discipline, and consistent effort, rather than avoiding difficulty.

18. Mojaddedi, *Masnavi*, 76.
19. Rumi, *Spiritual Couplets,* Book 1, Story 1.
20. "The True Sufi" trans. by R. A. Nicholson in Arberry, *Persian Poems.*

Rumi emphasizes that courage comes from within, not from external validation or the absence of fear. He encourages people to tap into their "inner knowing" and the intelligence of their bodies and souls. Instead of seeking an easy path, Rumi suggests that embracing challenges are part of a fulfilling life. He portrays courage as the ability to walk forward even when wounds are still healing. Rumi supports taking risks: a life without risk may result in nothing accomplished. Courage is also linked to living authentically and aligning with one's deepest truth. He encourages facing one's fear to gain strength and confidence. Rumi's message is that courage is an active, ongoing process of inner growth and a willingness to engage with life's complexities, leaving behind timidity:

> Respond to every call
> that excites your spirit.
> Ignore those that make you fearful
> and sad, that degrade you
> back toward disease and death.[21]

Rumi's philosophy encourages a fearless approach to life, suggesting that true existence is found in venturing beyond what is comfortable and familiar. It's about standing strong and being one's true self, unafraid to express passion and embrace individuality, even when life feels overwhelming. A daring life involves tuning into one's inner voice and letting it guide actions, rather than conforming to societal expectations or external rules. A courageous spirit requires setting aside negative influences and those who promote doubt.

> Run from what's comfortable. Forget safety. Live where you fear to live. Destroy your reputation. Be notorious. I have tried prudent planning long enough. From now on I'll be mad.
> Sell your cleverness and buy bewilderment.
> Your heart knows the way; run in that direction.
> Why do you stay in prison when the door is so wide open?[22]

Such lines encapsulate the idea of leaving safety for riskier, more profound experiences that lead to self-discovery. Rumi's daring language reveals a readiness to going beyond limits and beyond inherited constraints. For him, daring involves embracing wonder and the unknown. In his words

21. Barks, *Essential Rumi*, 156.

22. Barks, *Essential Rumi*, "A Community of the Spirit". For a cautious look at how Rumi can be uprooted from his Sufi context for western consumption see El-Zein, "Spiritual Consumption in the United States."

"Respond to every call that excites your spirit" Rumi urges us towards a life lived with joy and purpose.

RUMI SPEAKS

Evoking Mohammed's night journey and entry into heaven from the Jerusalem site we call the Dome of the Rock, when the Prophet was given the divine summons to *Salat* (prayer), Rumi, like Farid, writes of the ascent of the soul and the discovery of spiritual freedom in the experience of prayer:

> At every instant and from every side, resounds the call of Love:
> We are going to sky, who wants to come with us?
> We have gone to heaven, we have been the friends of the angels,
> And now we will go back there, for there is our country.
> We are higher than heaven, more noble than the angels:
> Why not go beyond them? Our goal is the Supreme Majesty.
> What has the fine pearl to do with the world of dust?
> Why have you come down here? Take your baggage back. What is this place?
> Luck is with us, to us is the sacrifice! . . .
>
> Like the birds of the sea, men come from the ocean—the ocean of the soul.
> How could this bird, born from that sea, make his dwelling here?
> No, we are the pearls from the bosom of the sea, it is there that we dwell:
> Otherwise how could the wave succeed to the wave that comes from the soul?
> The wave named "Am I not your Lord" has come, it has broken the vessel of the body;
> And when the vessel is broken, the vision comes back, and the union with Him.[23]

Rumi speaks often of longing—longing for home as a refugee, craving for lost love Shams. But his greatest yearning is for the Divine, for foretastes of heaven, of paradise on Earth. He likens his soul to a sighing flute:

> Hearken to the reed-flute, how it complains,
> Lamenting its banishment from its home:
> "Ever since they tore me from my osier bed,
> My plaintive notes have moved men and women to tears.

23. de Vitray-Meyerovitch, *Rumi and Sufism*, 48.

I burst my breast, striving to give vent to sighs,
And to express the pangs of my yearning for my home.
He who abides far away from his home
Is ever longing for the day he shall return.
My wailing is heard in every throng,
In concert with them that rejoice and them that weep.
Each interprets my notes in harmony with his own feelings,
But not one fathoms the secrets of my heart.
My secrets are not alien from my plaintive notes,
Yet they are not manifest to the sensual eye and ear.
Body is not veiled from soul, neither soul from body,
Yet no man hath ever seen a soul."
This plaint of the flute is fire, not mere air.
Let him who lacks this fire be accounted dead!
'Tis the fire of love that inspires the flute,
'Tis the ferment of love that possesses the wine.
The flute is the confidant of all unhappy lovers;
Yea, its strains lay bare my inmost secrets.
Who hath seen a poison and an antidote like the flute?
Who hath seen a sympathetic consoler like the flute?
The flute tells the tale of love's bloodstained path,
It recounts the story of my love toils.[24]

QUESTIONS FOR REFLECTION

1. Andrew Harvey writes:

> "Now Rumi is calling us to immense bravery. The only bravery that matters now is not something that only mystics need. Courage like this fueled Gandhi; courage like this fueled Martin King Jnr., courage like this fuels the inexhaustible passion of the Dalai Lama for peace. Unless we have this courage, unless we have this love, we are not going to be able to awaken the cynical and lost who are destroying the planet, or allowing it to be destroyed. . .We are not going to be bought, dismayed, or scared. We will be standing in the center of divine love, radiating divine love. . .We will need what Rumi has shown us. We will need to really root ourselves in divine passion and divine courage. . . How will we find the passion

24. Rumi, *Spiritual Couplets,* Book 1, Prologue.

> and the courage to save this world unless we know that this world is nothing less than a theophany of God?"[25]

What situations do you face, near or far, that require a courageous, risky response?

2. Rabia and Rumi were undeterred by convention, and pushed out the limits of language, using vocabulary others deemed risqué or outrageous. What risky action enthralls or entices you?
3. Rumi compares himself to a flute. If you were a musical instrument, which one might you be? Why?
4 What lines from Rabia surprise you or inspire you?
5. What resonances, parallels or contrasts do you see between this chapter's characters and Francis of Assisi?

FURTHER READING

Chittick, William C. *The Sufi Path of Love*. Albany: State University of New York Press, 1983.
Helminski, Kabir (Ed.) *The Rumi Collection*. Vermont: Threshold, 1988.
Lewis, F. D. *Rumi, Past, and Present, East and West*. Boston: Oneworld, 2001.
Nicholson, R. A. *Selected Poems from the Divan of Shams Tabrizi*. Maryland: IBEX, 2001.
Iqbal, Afzal. *The Life and Work of Jalal-ud-Din Rumi* . Islamic Book Trust, 2015.
Sapientia Mundi Press (anon). *The Wisdom of Rabia Al-Adawiyya: Divine Love, Holy Longing, and the Path of the Heart* (Sufi Wisdom Book 2).

25. Harvey, *Way of Passion*, 63.

Conclusion

Emerging Themes and Challenges

FOUR PARADOXES STAND OUT in the writings we have encountered: holy lives are worked out within the creative tension and energy of these paradoxes.

1 MIND AND HEART

A recurring theme in all traditions has been the interplay and complementarity of rational, analytical study and intuitive approaches to God—which we could sum up in the shorthand of "mind and heart".

First, we saw how Dominic was concerned that his religious brothers and sisters balanced study and service. He was more bookish than Francis who, we noted, famously wrote to Anthony of Padua: "It pleases me that you should teach sacred theology to the brothers as long as—in the words of the Rule—you 'do not extinguish the spirit of prayer and devotion with study of this kind.'"[1] The Dominicans made efforts to penetrate the universities, and went on to produce within a generation such great teachers as Thomas Aquinas (1225–1274)—a contemporary of Francis (just) who played his key role in developing Scholasticism, endeavoring to harmonize Aristotle's metaphysics and Latin theology.

In the Jewish tradition, we noticed a big contrast between Moses Maimonides and his son Abraham. Moses' treatise *The Guide for the Perplexed,* reconciled rational philosophy with religious faith. Abraham continued his father's rationalist tradition but also incorporated more mystical and pietistic elements into his thought, under the influence of Sufism. While

1. Armstrong et al, *Early Documents,* I:107.

his father emphasized a rather cerebral Aristotelian rationalism and Jewish law as pathways to God, Abraham leaned more toward spiritual experience, ethical self-refinement, and mystical devotion. We noted also Solomon Schechter's comments about "Nachmanides, the tender and compassionate, represented Judaism from the side of emotion and feeling, as Moses Maimonides did from the side of reason and logic."[2]

In the Islamic tradition contemporaneous with Francis we read of Ibn al-Arabi's distinction between the two types of traveler, the pilgrim and the academic. This is a call to live intuitively, imaginatively, not governed by rational, logical thought alone. It is an invitation to move beyond reason, which expresses itself in learned discourse, to poetry expressing the inexpressible in image and metaphor: a movement from analysis to awe, from explication to experience.

Islam holds together the two ways of thinking: the way of *Kalam* and the way of imagination. *Kalam* is the scholastic, speculative, or rational study of Islamic theology that analyzes the fundamental doctrines of Islamic faith, proving their validity, or refuting doubts regarding them rationally via logic. *Kalam* was born out of the need to establish and defend the tenets of Islam against philosophical doubters and non-Muslims. Chittick explains:

> If *Kalam* depended on reason to establish categories and distinctions, the Sufis depended on another faculty of the soul to bridge gaps and make connections. Many of them called this faculty "imagination" (*Khayah*)—the innate ability of the soul to perceive the presence of God in all things—a presence indicated by the Qu'ranic verse "Wherever you turn, there is the face of God" (2:115). The aim is reaching the stage of "unveiling" (*kashf*), the generic term for suprarational vision of God's presence in the world and in the soul. Ibn al-Arabi asserts that unveiling is a mode of knowledge superior to reason, but he also insists that reason provides the indispensable checks and balances without which it is impossible to differentiate among divine, angelic, psychic and satanic inrushes of imaginal knowledge.

He explains this in terms of two eyes

> The eye of imagination, unveiling, revels in God's presence and throws away all pretensions to logical precision. The eye of reason knows nothing of God's presence, because its analytical approach can only dissect endlessly. . .[3]

2. Schechter, "Nachmanides".
3. Chittick, *Sufism*, 30, 42.

Shifting Perceptions

In the time of Francis, the question of how we approach God, whether through intellectual inquiry or intuitive perception, was a live issue and indeed, resonates today, often in terms of intellectual/spiritual formation.

This can be traced through the question of how the clergy were prepared for ministry. Since the sixth century their formation was characterized by periods of residence in the bishop's household[4] or preparation under the auspices of monastic communities such as the Benedictines. But during the eleventh century theological schools attached to the cathedrals became more important than the monastic. Now, bishops created the post of chancellor for the express purpose of providing lectures for clergy. They hired teachers to equip the clergy with a basic Christian education: the training centered on the learning of Latin, familiarity with plainchant, and some basic mathematics to enable clerks to undertake parish book-keeping.[5] This shift from the Benedictines to institutional structures of the church, diocese and bishop was encouraged by Pope Gregory VII (Hildebrand, 1021–1085) as part of his reform program. This also included promoting a strictly celibate model of priesthood, conceived as a caste increasingly separate and removed from the laity.[6]

But the geographical shift from the monasteries of the countryside to the cathedral schools of the new towns represented a profounder change in the understanding and practice of theology, especially with the establishment of the first universities growing out of the episcopal schools in the twelfth century. Paris became a leading center for theological study at this time, paving the way for other large cities to develop autonomous universities, organizing their own curriculum and administration outside the structure of the Church. A gulf opened up between the study of theology and the life of the Church. Theology came to be studied as a separate discipline. This was encouraged by the new translations of Aristotle, and the analytical mode of theological enquiry that came to be called Scholasticism epitomized by Thomas Aquinas' *Summa Theologica* representing the attempt to defend Christian truth from the standpoint of reason.

4. The Council of Toledo in 531 required the instruction of ordinands "under the eyes of the bishop".

5. Moorman, *Church in England*, 87.

6. This was furthered by the Fourth Lateran Council of 1215 in its stress on the priestly powers of absolution. See Hughes, *Church in Crisis*.

Two different approaches to theology began to compete and theology itself came to be redefined. In patristic usage, *theologia* had referred to seeking a prayerful and inspired knowledge of God. It emphasized a personal and spiritual encounter with God rather than a purely intellectual or academic discipline. *Theologia* was intrinsically tied to spiritual experience, a communion with God that was considered the highest form of spiritual development.[7] Patristic *theologia* was not primarily an academic discipline but a deeper, more spiritual understanding that involved a rigorous engagement with Scripture and tradition.

But at the time of Francis and after, Thomas Aquinas and the Schoolmen, adapting an Aristotelian anthropology, developed theology as the systematic study of religion as a speculative and theoretical discipline, taking its place alongside law, physics and medicine in the university. Indeed theology becomes the "Queen of the sciences" viewed as a science, a body of knowledge or *scientia*, the Latin word *theologia* now taking on the meaning of "the discipline of sacred learning", with a clear emphasis on the systematic and academic study of the doctrinal aspects of faith.

In contrast, Franciscan thirteenth-century theologians such as Francis' contemporary Alexander of Hales (1185–1245)[8] and later John Duns Scotus (d. 1308), were concerned about the implications of neglecting the experiential side of theology. They advocated theology as a practical habit of the soul, a wisdom, inseparable from the practice of prayer and the virtues. For them, *habitus* is a divinely-given capacity arising from prayer. They understood theology as a *habitus* "an enduring orientation and dexterity of the soul . . . a cognitive disposition and orientation of the soul, a knowledge of God and what God reveals."[9]

Bonaventure (1217–74) advocated a mystical theory of knowledge stressing the priority of prayer in knowing God. He wrote:

> Let no one believe that he can be content with reading without inspiration, investigation without devotion, research without wonder, circumspection without exaltation, hard work without piety, knowledge without charity, intelligence without humility,

7. Certainly, patristic writers used contemporary philosophical concepts, particularly Platonic thought, to explore Christian understandings about God and the world.

8. The first Franciscan to hold a chair at the University of Paris, he taught Bonaventure.

9. Farley, *Theologia*, 35.

> zeal apart from divine grace, vision apart from divinely-inspired wisdom.[10]

Theological enquiry, as the serious and dedicated quest for God, was in danger of becoming separated from *ascesis*—the practice of prayer and spiritual disciplines that fostered a more intuitive approach to the Divine. Sheldrake puts it:

> The theological enterprise was no longer to be focused in centers that were explicitly dedicated to a religious way of life. The new scholarship in the narrow sense created centers that existed primarily to foster teaching and learning. The new theology gradually gave birth not only to distinctions between disciplines such as biblical theology, doctrinal theology and moral theology. It also produced a belief that the discipline of the mind could be separated from the discipline of an ordered lifestyle or *ascesis*.[11]

Orthodox theologian Vladimir Lossky expresses the inter-relation between theology and contemplative prayer:

> We must live the dogma expressing a revealed truth, which appears to us as an unfathomable mystery, in such a fashion that instead of assimilating the mystery to our mode of understanding, we should, on the contrary, look for a profound change, an inner transformation of spirit, enabling us to experience it mystically. Far from being mutually opposed, theology and mysticism support and complete each other. One is impossible without the other.[12]

More recently, Metropolitan Emilianos Timiados affirms:

> For the Fathers in general, theology is wholly a grace of God. God . . . is not a discernible object to be investigated, rather his life is a spiritual presence to be encountered. Theology then, is exclusively defined as a spiritual initiation . . .[13]

Thomas Merton calls for the flowing together of these two streams:

10. Cousins, *Bonaventure,* 55.

11. Sheldrake, *Spirituality and Theology,* 39.

12. Lossky, *Mystical Theology*, 8.

13. Timiados, "Theological Education and Spirituality", 21. He makes reference to Symeon the New Theologian, Gregory Nazianzus, Cyril of Alexandria. See also Arseniev, *Mysticism.*

> Learning has an important part to play in the contemplative life. . . Contemplation, far from being opposed to theology, is in fact the normal perfection of theology. We must not separate intellectual study of divinely revealed truth and contemplative experience of that truth as if they could never have anything to do with one another. On the contrary they are simply two aspects of the same thing. Dogmatic and mystical theology, or theology and spirituality are not to be set apart in mutually exclusive categories. . . This fallacious division perhaps explains much that is actually lacking both in theology and in spirituality. But the two belong together, just as body and soul belong together. Unless they are united, there is no fervor, no life and no spiritual value in theology, no substance, no meaning and no sure orientation in the contemplative life.[14]

Various perspectives cast light on the divide between theology and spirituality. McIntosh, who notes that "a large-scale historical analysis of this period of divorce remains to be written"[15] focuses on the increasing tendency towards individualism from the tenth century, and a movement towards the privatization of the mystical experience which had earlier been thought of as a corporate venture. He observes the growing medieval split between love and knowledge:

> By the later Middle Ages, the assumption has become in some cases nearly insurmountable that knowing is the task of theologians, while loving is a task for mystics; and instead of perceiving knowing and loving as one coherent activity in God, they come to appear as strangers, rivals, even enemies struggling for dominance in the drama of the inner self.[16]

Sheldrake writes about the divorce: "This division went deeper than method or content. It was, at heart, a division between the affective side of faith (or participation) and conceptual knowledge."[17] While scholars locate the divide as opening up with the development of the rational or scientific approach to theology advanced in Scholasticism, it is important not to lay the charge entirely at the feet of Aquinas, for he wrote out of the context of monastic spiritual disciplines.

14. Merton, *Seeds of Contemplation*, 197,198.
15. McIntosh, *Mystical Theology*, 63.
16. McIntosh, *Mystical Theology*, 71.
17. Sheldrake, *Spirituality and Theology*, 43.

Also within the Christian tradition we should recall Symeon the New Theologian (949–1022) wrote in the eleventh century (but from the Christian east, Constantinople) of *moving* or relocating the mind to the heart: "The mind should be in the heart. . .Keep your mind there (in the heart), trying by every possible means to find the place where the heart is, in order that, having found it, your mind should constantly abide there. Wrestling thus, your mind will find the place of the heart."[18]

Ware reminds us, in Orthodox theology: "the heart signifies the deep self; it is the seat of wisdom and understanding, the place where our moral decisions are made, the inner shrine in which we experience divine grace and the indwelling of the Holy Trinity. It indicates the human person as a spiritual subject, created in God's image and likeness."[19] Ware goes on: "Here is no head-heart dichotomy, for the intellect is *within* the heart. The heart is the meeting point between body and soul, between the subconscious, conscious and supraconscious, between the human and the divine."

Evagrius of Pontus (346–99) sums this up: "He who prays is a theologian; a theologian is one who prays."[20]

2 INTIMACY AND ULTIMACY

We encounter in all the traditions an intensity of love for God expressed in the sensuous language of union between the divine Bridegroom and human bride. The metaphor of the soul as bride, symbolizing deep love, faithfulness, and an intimate spiritual relationship with God, derives from the Hebrew tradition's *Song of Songs*. Originally appreciated as erotic poetry celebrating physical and embodied human love, its quickly became spiritualized: Jewish tradition interprets it as an allegory of the relationship between God and Israel, while Christianity sees it as an metaphor of the intense relationship between Christ and his bride the Church, or in individualized readings, of Christ and the soul.

Though this collection of love poems does not mention God, the divine presence is energizing the relationship. The Song not only uses erotic language, it also develops the theme of hide and seek, the presence and

18. Symeon the New Theologian, "Three Methods of Attention and Prayer" in Kadloubovsky & Palmer, *Writings From the Philokalia*, 158.

19. Ware, *Inner Kingdom*, 62.

20. Quoted, for example, in Louth, *Theology and Spirituality*, 4. I have explored this issue in depth in *Spirituality in Ministerial Formation*.

absence of the lover, so the emotions of both communion and distress are explored. It moves from lines like: "You have ravished my heart, my sister, my bride, you have ravished my heart with a glance of your eyes" (4:9), to "I sought him, but did not find him; I called him, but he gave no answer" (5:6).

Already in the Old Testament, as the relationship between Israel and her God was clarified in terms of a marriage covenant, erotic and sensual language communicates an intensity of desire in the heart of both parties. Indeed, the language of intimacy pervades the Old Testament. Daringly, God is depicted as a lover:

> As the bridegroom rejoices over the bride,
> so shall your God rejoice over you. (Isa 62:5)

At the time of Francis of Assisi this imagery was becoming popularized by the writings of Bernard of Clairvaux (1090–1153).[21] He traces a certain progression as he preaches on the topic "What it is to kiss the Lord's feet, hands and lips":

> This is the way and the order that must be followed. First, we fall at the feet of the Lord our Creator and lament our sins and faults. Second, we seek his helping hand to lift us up . . . Third . . . we may perhaps dare to lift up our eyes and view the Lord's glorious and majestic face. We are not only to adore him, but we are (and I say this with fear and trembling) to kiss him . . . made to be one Spirit in him.[22]

Richard of St Victor (1110–173) describes a "steep stairway of love" with four stages in the relationship: betrothal, corresponding with the stage of mystical purgation; courtship, which signifies mystical illumination; wedlock, the unitive stage; the fruitfulness of conjugal relations, where the mystic bride becomes "a parent of fresh spiritual life." Richard "saw clearly that the union of the soul with its Source could not be a barren ecstasy."[23] The key in his narrative is the redirecting of erotic passion towards God, which includes sometimes very vivid sexual, pregnancy, and birthing imagery.

21. Blackhouse, *Sermons of St Bernard of Clairvaux*, 34.

22. Blackhouse, *Sermons of St Bernard of Clairvaux*, 38.

23. Richard of St Victor, "The Four Degrees of Violent Charity", *Collected Works*, 140. "De Quatuor Gradibus Violentae Charitatis" (Migne, Patrologia Latina, vol. cxcvi. col. 1207). "De Quatuor Gradibus Violentae Charitatis" (Migne, Patrologia Latina, vol. cxcvi. col. 1207).

Clare of Assisi delights in this language:

> Draw me after You!
> We will run in the fragrance of Your perfumes,
> O heavenly Spouse!
> I will run and not tire,
> until You bring me into the wine-cellar,
> until Your left hand is under my head
> and Your right hand will embrace me happily
> and You will kiss me with the happiest kiss of Your mouth.[24]

She writes to Blessed Agnes of Prague:

> Queen and bride of Jesus Christ, look into the mirror daily and study well your reflection, that you may adorn yourself, mind and body, with an enveloping garment of every virtue, and thus find yourself attired in flowers and gowns befitting the daughter and most chaste bride of the King on high. In this mirror blessed poverty, holy humility and ineffable love are also reflected. With the grace of God the whole mirror will be your source of contemplation.[25]

Angela of Foligno (1248–1309) gives us another example of this language in the early Franciscan tradition. An Italian Franciscan tertiary, she describes how Christ touched her and embraced her whole being.

What of Francis himself? In his *Letter to all the Faithful*, Other becomes Brother, and Francis can hardly contain his excitement:

> We should never desire to be above others, but ought rather to be servants and subject "to every human creature for God's sake." And the Spirit of the Lord shall rest upon all those who do these things and persevere to the end, and He shall make His abode and dwelling in them.
>
> They shall be children of the heavenly Father whose works they do.
>
> They are the spouses, brothers and mothers of our Lord Jesus Christ.
>
> We are spouses [brides] when by the Holy Spirit the faithful soul is united to Jesus Christ.
>
> We are His brothers when we do the will of His Father who is in heaven.

24. Armstrong and Brady, *Francis and Clare,* 205.

25. Armstrong and Brady, *Francis and Clare,* 205.

> We are His mothers when we bear Him in our heart and in our body through pure love and a clean conscience and we bring Him forth by holy work which ought to shine as an example to others.
>
> O how glorious and holy and great to have a Father in heaven!
>
> O how holy, fair, and lovable to have a Spouse in heaven!
>
> O how holy and how beloved, well pleasing and humble, peaceful and sweet and desirable above all to have such a Brother who has laid down His life for His sheep. . .[26]

He uses the language of devotion to a feminine figure in various ways, transposing into a different key medieval romantic ideas of courtly and knightly love. First, Francis chooses a bride. The *Sacrum Commercium* (an early Franciscan treatise on Holy Poverty, c.1227) relates the allegory of Francis and some brothers climbing a mountain in search of a wondrous Woman:

> And so Lady Poverty greeted them with rich blessings: "Tell me brothers, what is the reason for your coming here and why do you come so quickly from the valley of sorrows to the mountain of light?" They answered: "We wish to become servants of the Lord of hosts because He is the King of glory. So, kneeling at your feet, we humbly beg you to agree to live with us and be our way to the King of glory, as you were the way when the dawn from on high came to visit those who sit in darkness and in the shadow of death."[27]

Second, Francis found much joy and encouragement in the person the Blessed Virgin Mary, who embodies for him the way of poverty and utter openness to God. Uniquely he hails her as "Virgin made Church"—seeing her as paradigm of Christian and Church. He exalts in her example in his *Salutation of the Blessed Virgin Mary*:

Hail, O Lady, Holy Queen,
Mary, holy Mother of God:
Virgin made Church
chosen by the most holy Father in heaven
consecrated with His most holy beloved Son
and with the Holy Spirit the Paraclete,
in whom there was and is
all the fullness of grace and every good.
Hail, His Palace!

26. Armstrong et al, *Early Documents,* I:49.
27. Armstrong et al, *Early Documents,* I:534.

Hail, His Tabernacle!
Hail, His Home!
Hail, His Robe!
Hail, His Servant!
Hail, His Mother!
Hail all you holy virtues
poured into the hearts of the faithful
through the grace and light of the Holy Spirit
so that from their faithless state
you may make them faithful to God.[28]

He no doubt has Mary in mind, then, in his poem *Salutation of the Virtues:*

Hail, Queen Wisdom, God salutes you
with your sister, holy pure Simplicity!
Lady, holy Poverty, God salutes you
with your sister, holy Humility!
Lady, holy Charity, God salutes you
with your sister, holy Obedience!
Holy Virtues, all be saluted by God
from Whom you come and proceed. . .[29]

The use of bridal imagery is all the more striking in the Islamic tradition which emphasizes the transcendence and Otherness of God. We have seen language both tender and outrageous in the writings of Rabia, Rumi and Ibn al-Farid. There are a few references in the Qur'an to the closeness of God—famously, "I am nearer to you than your jugular vein"—but the overwhelming sense of God is One who as Absolute Judge dwells in faraway heavens. On the contrary, our Sufi writers urge us to risk intimacy with God, lowering our self-protective barriers and feeling his breath upon our skin.

3 ACTION AND CONTEMPLATION

One of the fundamental paradoxes in the spiritual life is the interplay or conflict between stillness and movement. Some people feel torn apart between the call of duty and the call to prayer. They find themselves constantly juggling competing commitments to family and work with the need for rest and renewal. This struggle is compounded by guilt or a sense of failure. If we end up compartmentalizing life—in order to safeguard stillness or

28. Armstrong et al, *Early Documents,* I:163.

29. Armstrong et al, *Early Documents,* I:164.

commitment in the world—we run the risk of a "split spirituality"[30] or the dichotomy of living a divided life, pulled back and forth between prayer and action. What wisdom do our writers have to offer?

Francis' Dilemma

First, we recall that Francis himself had wrestled over the question of the relationship between activity and stillness and found himself torn between the two, as Bonaventure relates in his biography. Francis agonizes:

> What do you think, brothers, what do you judge better? That I should spend my time in prayer, or that I should travel about preaching? . . . in prayer there seems to be a profit and an accumulation of graces, but in preaching a distribution of gifts already given from heaven.

He went on to rehearse the advantages of a life dedicated solely to prayer:

> In prayer there is a purification of interior affections and a uniting to the one, true and supreme good with an invigorating of virtue; in preaching, there is dust on our spiritual feet, distraction over many things and a relaxation of discipline.

Ultimately he sees the truth that proves to be decisive:

> There is one thing . . . that seems to outweigh all these considerations before God, that is, the only begotten Son of God, who is the highest wisdom, came down from the bosom of the Father for the salvation of souls in order to instruct the world by his example and to speak the word of salvation to people . . . holding back for himself absolutely nothing that he could freely give for our salvation. And because we should do everything according to the pattern shown us in him . . . it seems more pleasing to God that I interrupt my quiet and go out to labor.[31]

According to *The Little Flowers of St Francis* (ch. 16) Sister Clare and Brother Silvester, after a time of prayer, agree on the same advice to Francis: "Continue with your preaching, because God called you not for your sake alone but for the salvation of others."[32] However, in the life of Francis, this was never going to be an "either/or" choice. In the course of his mission, he

30. Rolheiser, *Seeking Spirituality*.

31. Armstrong et al, *Early Documents*, II: 622.

32. Blaiklock & Keys, *Little Flowers*, 54.

established hermitages and retreats, and his whole ministry was an ebb and flow of action and contemplation. He models an integration of prayer into service, an inter-penetration and cross-fertilization between the two. It has been written of Francis: "his mystical experience, far from cutting him off from the world, always sent him right back into its most basic realities."[33] Francis knew that the presence of God was not only to be found in stillness and solitude, but, as also in the despised leper and the feared wolf.

Francis composed *A Rule for Hermitages* showing that he values solitude amidst activity. In this text Francis puts only one biblical text. It related to the Kingdom: "And let them seek first of all the Kingdom of God and his justice" (Matt 6:33).[34]

Francis' life of witness culminated in the experience of receiving the stigmata on Mt Alverna: the very wounds of Christ appeared in his own feet, hands and side. But this was not a private ecstasy. Rather, Bonaventure tells us in his *Major Legend,* it led Francis to fresh engagement with the lepers. He continued to say to his brothers "Let us begin, brothers, to serve the Lord our God, for up to now we have done little." Bonaventure tells us: "He burned with a great desire to return to the humility he preached at the beginning; to nurse lepers as he did at the outset."[35] This encapsulates Francis' testimony: the experience of prayer enabled a life marked by reaching out to others.

Francis no doubt would agree with Albert in the values he embodied in his *Rule*, though Francis lived as a pilgrim and mendicant on the road while Albert wrote for settled hermits. Francis would concur with Albert's keen sense of the need for balance between solitude and community, work and prayer, activity and rest, silence and talking, sharing of resources and having only what is needful.

The Jewish tradition is rich in exemplars of the contemplative/active life. Moses, while at work tending flocks, glimpsed the Divine in a bush alight, and went alone into the darkness and cloud atop Sinai, returning to lead thousands forward in their journey. Elijah followed an exhausting life, and came to realize on the same mount the necessity of listening out for the "still small voice of calm" amidst the noise of earthquake and wind and fire (1 Kgs 19:11–13). Abraham Maimonides refers to their examples: "Solitude

33. Rotzetter et al, *Gospel Living*, 180.

34. Merton, *Contemplation in a World of Action*, 263, 264.

35. Armstrong et al, *Early Documents*, II: 640. See also Jordan, *Affair of the Heart*, 51,52.

is among the most distinguished of the elevated paths. It is moreover the way of the very great saints and by it the prophets achieved union with God." We noted his useful distinction between *outward solitude*—physical seclusion from distractions to quieten the senses, and *inward solitude*—a focus completely on God. Here is the interplay between stillness of body and soul. We saw that Abraham never advocated a monastic type of seclusion, but like his father, he saw as important engagement with the world, family, and community. Solitude was meant to be temporary and purposeful, a cherished element somehow squeezed into, for Abraham, his jostling commitments as physician, religious and political leader, scholar, husband and father.

But can this lead to a divided life, wrestled between conflicting demands? We may find ourselves vacillating between alternatives, trying to find room for each competing need, establishing rhythms and patterns of life permitting a sometimes uncomfortable co-existence between competing elements of stillness vs. movement, hospitality vs. solitude. Is it possible not only to achieve some sort of resolution between demands clamoring for attention but rather, at the very center of our being, to unify and weld together the stillness and action, the listening and speaking, where contemplation and action become integrated, part of one another?

Nachmanides gives us clues to such a life in his call for us to live with an alertness ready to discern and celebrate God's "natural miracles" everywhere. He saw God at work moment by moment in creation. We saw how he urges us to live at all times and in all places with faith and trust: with *Emunah,* a comprehensive awareness that God is present and active in all aspects of life, and with *Bitachon,* the calm confidence that lets go of fear, because one holds onto the sense that God is in control, trusting that nothing happens by chance.

Ibn al-Arabi maybe holds the secret to becoming a contemplative in action, with his call for us to live with our imaginative faculty switched on so we go about our business in constant awareness of the Divine Presence. Nor do we forget that Sufis valued solitude or retreat (*khalwa*) as a central practice to engender purification of the heart, remembrance of God (*dhikr*), and the mystical union with the Divine.

Rumi's life in Konya was at times hectic, complex and demanding. He worked as an Islamic jurist, issuing legal rulings (*fatwas*). He also served as a *molvi* (Islamic teacher), teaching students in the *madrasa* and giving sermons in the mosques of the city, not to mention producing his immense literary output. Yet Ruhl tells us:

> Though Rumi's immense outpouring of more than 35,000 poems constitute a remarkable gushing and surging of language, Rumi also professes to value silence when prolixity [wordiness] threatens to blunt his raw contact with Reality, or when he encounters the ineffable.[36]

Rumi celebrates silence:

> This silence, this moment, every moment, if it's genuinely inside you, brings what you need. There's nothing to believe. Only when I stopped believing in myself did I come into this beauty. Sit quietly, and listen for a voice that will say, "Be more silent." Die and be quiet. Quietness is the surest sign that you've died. Your old life was a frantic running from silence. Move outside the tangle of fear-thinking. Live in silence . . .[37]
>
> All is known in the sacredness of silence.
> Silence is the language of God, all else is poor translation.[38]

In the Christian tradition we speak of sacramental looking: discerning signs of God's presence everywhere, ruling nothing out. We seek to overcome the dichotomy of contemplation vs. action by seeing God in all things and at all times. With Francis and Hildegard we delight in the world as God-bearing and God-revealing—indeed, we hail the world as sacrament.

Hildegard looked at the fields, trees and plants and saw there messages about the greening and wetness of the soul. The recognition of the interconnectedness of all things in God's world enabled Francis to live with a keen sense of God's presence and providence. He was not so much a nature mystic, as he has been called, but a natural mystic, attuned to living a contemplative life everyday and in every context, not only in the hermitage but walking the lanes of the countryside and streets of the city. In his *Canticle of Creation* Francis looked at the four elements—earth, water, air, fire—and greeted them as brother and sister:

> Praise God, Brother Wind!
> Through air, cloudy and serene, every kind of weather,
> God gives sustenance to all creatures.
> Praise God, Sister Water!

36. Ruhl, *Enlightened Contemporaries*, 123.
37. Rumi, *"This silence, this moment"*.
38. Kononenko, *Teachers of Wisdom*, 134.

God made you useful, humble, precious and chaste.
Praise God, Brother Fire!
In you, beautiful, playful, robust and strong,
God lights the night.
Praise God, our Sister Mother Earth!
You govern and sustain us,
with fruit and colors, flowers and herbs.[39]

For Christians, this resonates with the teaching of Jean-Pierre de Caussade (1675–1751) in his influential work *Abandonment to Divine Providence*. His central teaching is "the sacrament of the present moment." God is present and active in every moment, and daily life is the vehicle of divine grace: "The present moment is always full of infinite treasures; it contains more than you are capable of receiving."[40]

4 CONTEXT AND LIFESTYLE

Living with Faith in Uncertain Times

All our writers lived in situations marked by conflict, struggle and fear.

Francis served as a soldier in the wars between city states (Assisi vs. Perugia), and regularly encountered the conflict between church and state, pope vs. emperor. Hildegard confronted rejection and experienced struggles with bishops and popes.

Jews and Muslims who lived on the Iberian peninsula in the 12th and 13th centuries encountered waves of persecution as the Christians sought to advance their *Reconquista*. Jews faced violent outbreaks of antisemitism. Nachmanides faced personal opposition and was forced to leave Spain. In the Rhinelands, Eleazar saw his wife and children slaughtered by fanatics before his very eyes.

Rumi fled Mongol terror as a child and young man, becoming a refugee, repeatedly displaced further and further from his homeland.

All revealed a tenacity of soul as they sought to live counter-cultural, prophetic lives. Their varied lives illustrate different pathways to holiness, different lifestyles with similar values.

They were people of perseverance who never gave up. Their bold vision didn't come cheap for it was forged in the crucible of suffering, whether

39. Armstrong et al, *Early Documents*, I:113.

40. Muggeridge, *Sacrament of the Present Moment*.

personal or societal. Their faith, though taking quite different forms, enabled them to withstand loss and challenge. They were prepared to move—physically and spiritually—and to venture into new lands, be it Egypt, Asia Minor or other parts of Europe. This outward readiness to overcome barriers and go beyond limits revealed a largeness of spirit capable of quitting spiritual comfort zones and live with risk. They were people of nerve and verve. Across the centuries they call out to us: never underestimate yourself! Transcend your limits! Realize your God-given potential!

FOUR SHARED IMPERATIVES

As we seek to respond to our own context and the needs around us, we might hold onto abiding and perennial values that guided Francis' Christian and interfaith contemporaries. Four common virtues shine out and radiate different aspects of holiness across this spiritual galaxy.

Respond to Your Context with Compassion

Francis reveals the grace of compassion in his active kindness to the poor, marginalized, and even animals: when he embraces a leper, picks up a worm from the road so it will not be trod upon. In Francis, compassion is a deep, transformative outlook that extends to all of God's creation, rooted in his personal experience of God's mercy and his simple, humble lifestyle. He embodied a loving, all-encompassing empathy that sees every living thing as a reflection of the Creator. His approach to compassion includes respecting the dignity of every person, offering hospitality, and showing mercy to all, including enemies:

> The friars should be delighted to follow the lowliness and poverty of our Lord Jesus Christ, remembering that of the whole world we must own nothing; "but having food and sufficient clothing, with these let us be content", as St Paul says (1 Tim 6:8). They should be glad to live among social outcasts, among the poor and helpless, the sick and the lepers, and those who beg by the wayside. The friars should have no hesitation about telling one another what they need, so that they can provide for one another. They are bound to love and care for one another as brothers, according to the means God gives them, just as a mother loves and cares for her son. . .

> Remember the words of our Lord, "Love your enemies, do good to those who hate you" (Mt. 5:44). Our Lord Jesus Christ himself, in whose footsteps we must follow (1 Pet. 2:21), called the man who betrayed him his friend, and gave himself up of his own accord to his executioners. Therefore, our friends are those who for no reason cause us trouble and suffering, shame or injury, pain or torture, even martyrdom and death. It is these we must love, and love very much, because for all they do to us we are given eternal life. . .[41]

Dominic echoes this message when he writes "I leave you first, charity; I leave you, secondly, humility; lastly, I leave you voluntary poverty." We noted how he suggested to the powers that be that they get down from their high-horse and start to walk alongside people. This was his way.

We notice the combination of humility and compassion in the Jewish stars in this firmament. Abraham Maimonides, extolling generosity and gentleness, quotes the Torah: "Rejoice in all the good the Lord your God has given you: you, and the stranger that is in the midst of you" (Deut 26:11). The early Hasidics lived a disciplined and self-denying life, so as to be available to their neighbors in need, as outlined in the *Sefer Hasidim.*

Respond to Your Context with Contemplation

In all traditions, we noticed a deep desire to cultivate a sense of the Sacred, and to live in a contemplative awareness before God. The German Hasidic Eleazar of Worms urges people to live with reverence on earth: "The secret is reverence of the Lord."

Farid encourages us to live as a pilgrim, wherever on earth we may be dwelling:

> Any place that holds the Beloved
> is a precinct holy;
> every house where she resides
> is Medina.
> Wherever she dwells
> is Jerusalem, most sacred,
> whose soothing sight
> cools my burning heart.[42]

41. Habig, *English Omnibus of Sources,* Rule of 1221.

42. Homerin, *Sufi Verse, Saintly Life,* 177.

We nurture a sense of the sacred when we recognize "thin places" can be anywhere and everywhere: the unveiling might happen at any time!

Ibn al-Arabi considers this in terms of a lifting of veils (*kashf*) that separate the seeker from the true Reality. Unveiling is not just a mystical experience but a way of knowing: a direct perception of divine truths, the immediate, experiential knowledge of God, surpassing the limits of reason. The heart (*qalb*) is the locus of unveiling. Purified, it reflects divine realities like a polished mirror. Ultimately this leads to the unveiling of *Unity*, where the seeker perceives all existence as a manifestation of the One Being. In words attributed to Rumi:

> I said: what about my eyes?
> *God said: Keep them on the road.*
> I said: what about my passion?
> *God said: Keep it burning.*
> I said: what about my heart?
> *God said: Tell me what you hold inside it?*
> I said: pain and sorrow.
> *He said: Stay with it. The wound is the place where the Light enters you.*[43]

The common aim is to walk with humility and tread gently upon the Earth.

Respond to Your Context with Creativity

These voices from the time of Francis beseech us: celebrate your creativity and God-given potential!

Hildegard urges us to live with awareness of the Divine, delighting in the signs of God's presence, like the dew on the wet grass and the greening of the planet. She calls out to us: Refuse to be constrained by others! Unleash your creativity—to the greater glory of God. Don't let your wings be clipped! Fly, as you were destined to do! Rumi echoes these sentiments:

> You were born with potential. You were born with goodness and trust. You were born with ideals and dreams. You were born with greatness. You were born with wings. You are not meant for crawling, so don't. You have wings. Learn to use them and fly.[44]

43. Rumi, "I said: what about my eyes".
44. Rumi, "You Were Born with Potential".

We can be ready to learn from other traditions, too, like Abraham Maimonides as he incorporated Islamic Sufi practices into his spiritual disciplines, as we believe Francis modelled his *Praises of God* on the Islamic litany of the divine names.

Respond to Your Context with Courage

What radiates in these holy lives is a sense of faith, perseverance and determination in tough times. All our stars glow with courage (lit. heart), and with a confidence which, of course literally means "with faith." Al-Farid reveals an outlook undeterred by hardships:

> Plant yourself firm
> and flourish. . .
>
> Be sharp and hard as time itself,
> for hate is the fate of "maybe,"
> and beware of "perhaps,"
> a most dangerous disease.
>
> Strand straight, try to please the Beloved;
> push yourself hard, do not waver,
> and never give in
> to a sudden passing weakness.
>
> Though crippled, walk;
> though broken
> do not defer
> your firm resolve.
>
> Lead the way, charge ahead,
> for you prepared for this. . .
>
> Slash with the sword of determination
> any talk of future;
> if you are steadfast, you will find freedom,
> for the sacrificing soul strives on![45]

Hildegard heartens us:

45. Homerin, *Umar Ibn al-Farid,* 125–27.

Humankind should ponder God. . .
recognize God's wonders and signs.
Let these signs and wonders be
the firmament on which to build,
so as not to be shaken by fear,
or distracted from the love
of God. . .
Now here is the image of the power
of God:
This firmament is an all-encompassing
circle.
No one can say where this wheel begins
or ends.[46]

And Francis, once again, calls us to look heavenward and celebrate the stars in the galaxy:

Most High, all-powerful, good Lord,
Yours are the praises, the glory, and the honor, and all blessing. . .
Praised be You, my Lord, with all Your creatures,
especially Sir Brother Sun,
who is the day and through whom You give us light.
He is beautiful and radiant with great splendor;
and bears a likeness of You, Most High One.
Praised be You, my Lord, through Sister Moon and the stars,
in heaven You formed them clear and precious and beautiful. . .
Praise and bless my Lord and give Him thanks
and serve Him with great humility![47]

A time of uncertainty, overshadowed by fear and war, by darkness punctuated with sparks of faith, glimmers of renewal: not only the twelfth and thirteen centuries, but the 21st century too. May these eternal stars in the firmament inspire us to live lives of glowing faith, bringing hope to others. And in a divided, polarized world these stars which share a common firmament urge us to reach out to one other across the spaces that separate us, learn from and encourage one other, and share our God-given light!

46. Uhlein, *Meditations*, 45, 29.

47. Armstrong et al, *Early Documents*, I:113.

Appendix

Responding with the Heart

THESE GUIDELINES WORK FOR both normal study groups of a single religion, and inter-religious gatherings. Our interfaith group in Jerusalem consisted of two or three Christians, and the same number of Jews and Muslims, about 9 people in total. For each monthly meeting one person was asked to select a piece of work to share with the group: this could be a reading from scripture, a poem or a piece of prose, or it could even be a picture or an art object. People's initial reactions to the chosen piece of work were shared—how it strikes them—and then more reflective, engaging "responses from the heart" were disclosed, forming part of a gentle discussion during which people were able to speak freely. We had a sense that a sacred space opened up in the course of our hour's meeting. Here is the "Mutual Invitation Format" used in Jerusalem interfaith gatherings:

1. The leader has chosen a short reading from Sacred Scripture or spiritual writing, poem, etc.
2. The leader reads the chosen work aloud.
3. The leader invites someone (it needn't be in any particular order) to respond with a word or phrase which is their initial response to the reading. They do not explain or justify their choice to the group, and the group does not remark or question this word. They simply listen. That person then invites the response of another group member until

all who wish have spoken. Anyone can pass at any time if they are not ready to share a word/phrase for whatever reason. It is not necessary to explain why. The leader responds last.

4. The text is read again, this time by a second member of the group. The original leader will add a specific question to reflect on concerning the text. It could simply be a general question such as "What insights come up for you?" or "What does this text say to us today in our present situation?"

5. The reader invites a member to respond. This should be a relatively short (one or two minutes) response from the heart, not a theological, academic dissertation. If someone goes on and on, the leader can gently remind him/her of the time restraints. The leader should give their reflections last since they are most familiar with the text. At this time, there is no interruption or discussion. Everyone simply listens to each other.

   If desired, and with agreement of the whole group, a discussion can continue following this initial reflection.

6. The text is read for a third and final time by a new person. This time it is read as a prayer and the group simply listens.

Bibliography

Adlerblum, Nima Hischensohn. "Reinterpretation of Jewish Philosophy". *Journal of Philosophy, Psychology and Scientific Methods* 14:7 (1917) 181–89. doi.org/10.2307/2940717

Akkach, Samer. "The World of Imagination in Ibn Al-Arabi's Ontology". *British Journal of Middle Eastern Studies* 24:1 (1997) 97–113. scholar.google.com/citations?view_op=view_citation&hl=en&user=xiyXLjEAAAAJ&citation_for_view=xiyXLjEAAAAJ:d1gkVwhDploC

Arabi, Ibn. *The Alchemy of Human Happiness.* Part of *Meccan Illuminations (al-Futuḥat al-Makkiyya)*, translated by Stephen Hirtenstein. Oxford: Anqa, 2017.

Arberry Arthur J., ed. *Persian Poems: An Anthology of Verse Translations.* New York: Everyman's Library, 1972.

Armstrong, Regis J., Hellman, Wayne, and Short, William J., eds. *Francis of Assisi Early Documents (3 vols.)* New York: New City, 2000.

Armstrong, Regis J. and Brady, Ignatius C., trans. *Francis and Clare: The Complete Works.* New York: Paulist, 1986.

Arseniev, Nicolas. *Mysticism and the Eastern Church.* London: Mowbrays, 1979.

Attar, Farid al-Din, *Memorial of God's Friends: Lives and Sayings of Sufis. Tadhkirat al-Awliya* (*Lives of the Saints*) translated by Paul Losensky. New York: Paulist, 2009.

Barks, Coleman. *The Essential Rumi.* San Francisco: HarperOne, 2022.

Blackhouse, Halcyon, ed. *The Song of Songs: Sections from the Sermons of St Bernard of Clairvaux.* London: Hodder & Stoughton, 1990.

Blaiklock, E.M., and Keys A. C., trans. *The Little Flowers of St Francis.* London: Hodder & Stoughton, 1985.

Block, Tom. "Abraham Maimonides: A Jewish Sufi". *Sufi Magazine* (2001).

Bowie, Fiona, and Davies, Oliver, eds. *Hildegard of Bingen: An Anthology.* London: SPCK, 1990.

Butcher, Carmen Acevedo. *Incandescence: 365 Readings with Women Mystics.* Orleans, MA: Paraclete, 2005.

———. *St. Hildegard of Bingen: Doctor of the Church; A Spiritual Reader.* Orleans, MA: Paraclete, 2013.

Byrne, Lavinia. *Traditions of Spiritual Guidance.* London: Geoffrey Chapman, 1990.

Calabria, Michael D. “Ibn al-Farid: Francis’ Sufi Contemporary”. *Spirit and Life* 13 *Mirroring One Another, Reflecting the Divine: the Franciscan-Muslim Journey into God* (2009) 53–73.

———. “Introducing the Sultan al-Malik al-Kamil”, *Colloquium Sancte Franciscii Cum Sultano: St. Francis and the Sultan, 1219–2019*. Cincinnati, OH: Franciscan Media.

Caravella, Miriam Bokser. *The Mystic Heart of Judaism*. Radha Soami Satsang Beas, 2011. rssb.org/the-mystic-heart-of-judaism15.html?

Chittick, William C. “Ibn al-Arabi: The Doorway to an Intellectual Tradition”. *Journal of the Journal of the Muhyiddin Ibn Al-Arabi Society* 59 (2016). ibnarabisociety.org/doorway-to-an-intellectual-tradition-william-chittick.

———. *Sufism*. Oxford: Oneworld, 2000.

Ciabattari, Jane. “Why is Rumi the best-selling poet in the US?” bbc.com/culture.

Cousins, Ewert, trans. *Bonaventure: The Soul’s Journey into God*. London: SPCK, 1978.

Craine, Renate. *Hildegard: Prophet of the Cosmic Christ*. New York: Crossroad, 1998.

Custato, Michael F. *Francis of Assisi: His Life, Vision, and Companions*. London: Reaktion, 2023.

Dan, Joseph, ed. *The Early Kabbalah*. New York: Paulist, 1986.

Dannhausen, Barbara, and Poochigian, Ruth. “Dominic’s charism”. Dominican Mission and Heritage, 2003. sinsinawa.org.

Dominic, “Last Will and Testament”. vanvick.wordpress.com/2011/04/19/the-last-will-and-testament-of-st-dominic/

El-Zein, Amira. “Spiritual Consumption in the United States: The Rumi phenomenon.” *Islam and Christian–Muslim Relations* 11:1 (2010) 71–85.

Farley, Edward. *Theologia: the Fragmentation and Unity of Theological Education*. Minneapolis, MN: Augsburg Fortress, 1983.

Fenton, Paul B. “Abraham ben Moses Maimonides,” in *Encyclopedia of the Bible and its Reception, Vol. 1*, 215–16. Berlin: de Gruyter, 2009.

Fox, Matthew. *Hildegard of Bingen’s Book of Divine Works*. Sante Fe, NM: Bear & Co., 1987.

———. *Illuminations of Hildegard of Bingen*. Santa Fe: Bear & Co., 2003.

Fry, Timothy, trans. *The Rule of St Benedict*. Collegeville, MN: Liturgical, 1980.

García-Serrano, Francisco, ed., *The Friars and their Influence in Medieval Spain*. Amsterdam: University Press, 2018.

Gooch, Brad. *Rumi’s Secret: The Life of the Sufi Poet of Love*. San Francisco: Harper Perennial, 2018.

Habig, Marion A., ed. *English Omnibus of Sources: Writings and Early Biographies*. Chicago: Franciscan Herald, 1973.

Hadewijch. *The Complete Works*. Translated by Columba Hart. New York: Paulist, 1980.

Halligan, F.R. “The Creative Imagination of the Sufi Mystic, Ibn Al-Arabi.” *Journal of Religion and Health* 40 (2001) 275–87.

Harvey, Andrew. *The Way of Passion: A Celebration of Rumi*. London: Penguin, 2000.

Helminski, Camille Adams. *Women of Sufism: A Hidden Treasure*. Boulder, Colorado: Shambhala, 2003.

Hershler, D., trans. *Sefer Rokeach*. Jerusalem: Mossad HaRav Kook, 1960.

Heywood, W., trans. *The Little Flowers of St. Francis*. JollyJoy, 2004 [reprint of 1906]. sacred-texts.com.

Hildegard of Bingen. *Scivias*. Translated by Mother Columba Hart. New York: Paulist, 1990.

Homerin, Th. Emil, *Passion Before Me, My Fate Behind: Ibn al-Farid and the Poetry of Recollection*. State University of New York Press, 2011.

———. *Umar Ibn al-Farid: Sufi Verse, Saintly Life*. New York: Paulist, 2001.

Hughes, Phillip. *The Church in Crisis: The Twenty Great Councils*. London: Burns & Oates, 1961.

Jordan, Pauline. *An Affair of the Heart: a Biblical and Franciscan Journey*. Leominster: Gracewing, 2008.

Kononenko, Igor. trans. *Teachers of Wisdom*. Pittsburgh, PA: Dorrance, 2010. Azquotes.com.

Ladinsky, Daniel, trans. *Poems From God: Inspirations from Twelve Sacred Voices of the East and West*. London: Penguin, 2002.

Lossky, Vladimir. *The Mystical Theology of the Eastern Church*. Cambridge: James Clarke, 1957.

Louth, Andrew. *Theology and Spirituality*. Oxford: SLG, 1976.

Maimonides, Moses. *Epistulae*. Edited by David Hirsch Baneth. Jerusalem: Magnes, 1985.

Mandonnet, Pierre. *St. Dominic and His Work*. Translated by Sister Mary Benedicta Larkin, O.P. St. Louis: Herder, 1948.

Marcus, Ivan G., trans. "Mothers, Martyrs, and Moneymakers: Some Jewish Women in Medieval Europe". *Conservative Judaism* 8:3 (1986).

Margaliot, Mordecai, trans. *Sefer Ha-razim*. Jerusalem: American Academy for Jewish Research, 1966. archive.org.

Massignon, Louis. *Hallaj: Mystic and Martyr*. Princeton: University Press, 1982.

Mayes, Andrew D. *Gateways to the Divine: Transformative Pathways of Prayer from the Holy City of Jerusalem*. Euguene, OR: Wipf and Stock, 2019.

———. *Spirituality in Ministerial Formation: The Dynamic of Prayer in Learning*. Cardiff: University of Wales Press, 2009.

McIntosh, Mark A. *Mystical Theology: The Integrity of Spirituality and Theology*. Oxford: Blackwell, 1998.

Merton, Thomas. *Contemplation in a World of Action*. London: George Allen & Unwin, 1971.

———. *Seeds of Contemplation*. Wheathampstead: Anthony Clarke, 1972.

Mojaddedi, Jawid, trans. *The Masnavi by Jalal al-Din Rumi*. Oxford: OUP, 2025.

Moorman, John R.H. *A History of the Church in England*. London: Adam & Charles Black, 1958.

———. *A History of the Franciscan Order*. Oxford: Clarendon, 1968.

Morris, James Winston. "The Spiritual Ascension: Ibn Arabi and the Miraj. Pt. 1". *Journal of the American Oriental Society* 107 (1987) 629–52.

Muggeridge, Kitty. *Sacrament of the Present Moment*. London: Fount, 1982.

Nachmanides. *Commentary on the Torah*. Translated by Charles B. Chavel. New York: Shilo, 1973. sefaria.org.

———. *Iggeret HaRamban* (Ramban's Letter). sefaria.org.

Naqshbandi Haqqani Rabbani, "Umar-Ibn-al-Farid". Amsterdam, Netherlands: sufipathoflove.com/umar-ibn-al-farid/.

Obbard, Elizabeth Ruth. *Land of Carmel*. Leominster: Gracewing, 1999.

Richard of St Victor. *Collected Works*. NC: Revelation Insight/Lulu, 2015.

Rolheiser, Ronald. *Seeking Spirituality*. London: Hodder & Stoughton, 1998.

Rosenblatt, Samuel, trans. *The High Ways to Perfection of Abraham Maimonides. Vol 1*. New York: Columbia University Press, 1927. archive.org.

Rotzetter, A., Van Dijk W.-C. and Matura, T. *Gospel Living: Francis of Assisi Yesterday and Today.* New York: Franciscan Institute, 1994.

Ruhl, Steve K. *Enlightened Contemporaries: Francis, Dogen, and Rumi: Three Great Mystics of the Thirteenth Century and Why They Matter Today.* Rhinebeck, NY: Monkfish, 2020.

Rumi, Jalaluddin. "I said: what about my eyes". azquotes.com/quote/856212

———. *The Masnavi: The Spiritual Couplets.* Translated by E.H. Whinfield (1898).
archive.sacred-texts.com/isl/masnavi/msn01.htm

———. "This silence, this moment". azquotes.com/quote/566950

———. "You Were Born with Potential". yourdailypoem.com/listpoem.jsp?poem_id=4736

Russ-Fishbane, Elisha. *Judaism, Sufism, and the Pietists of Medieval Egypt: A Study of Abraham Maimonides and His Times.* Oxford: Oxford University Press 2015.

Savedow, Steve, trans. *The Book of the Angel Reziel.* York Beach, ME: Weiser, 2000. archive.org.

Schechter, Solomon. "Nachmonides" *The Jewish Quarterly Review* 5:1 (1892) 18–23.

Sheldrake, Philip. *Spirituality and History.* London: SPCK, 1991.

———. *Spirituality and Theology: Christian Living and the Doctrine of God* London: Darton, Longman & Todd, 1998.

Sholem, Gershom. *Major Trends in Jewish Mysticism.* New York: Schocken, 1946.

———. *On the Kabbalah and its Symbolism.* New York: Schocken, 1960.

Smelt, Joachim. *The Carmelites.* Darien, IL: Carmelite Spiritual Center, 1988.

Soskice, Janet. *Sisters of Sinai.* London: Vintage, 2010.

Southern, Richard W. *The Making of the Middle Ages.* London: Pimlico, 1993.

Sapienta Mundi, *The Wisdom of Ibn Al-Arabi: Unity of Being, Divine Imagination, and the Secrets of the Cosmos.* 2025.

Shah, Idries. *The Sufis.* London: ISF, 2015.

Smith, Paul, trans. *Diwan of Ibn Al-Farid.* Campbells Creek, Victoria: New Humanity, 2018.

Society of St Francis, Third Order. *Living with the Principles of the Order.* Hilfield, Dorset: Society of St Francis, 2005.

Symeon the New Theologian. "Three Methods of Attention and Prayer" in E. Kadloubovsky and G.E.H. Palmer, *Writings From the Philokalia.* London: Faber & Faber, 1977.

Teresa of Avila. *Interior Castle.* Translated by E. Allison Peers. London: Sheed and Ward, 1974.

Tobin, Frank, trans. *Mechthild of Magdeburg: The Flowing Light of the Godhead.* New York: Paulist, 1998.

Tugwell, Simon, trans. *Nine Ways of Prayer of Saint Dominic.* Dublin: Dominican, 1978.

Timiados, Emilianos. "Theological Education and Spirituality." *Ministerial Formation* 30 (1985) 21.

Uhlein, Gabriele. *Meditations with Hildegard of Bingen.* Sante Fe, NM: Bear & Co., 1982.

Upton, Charles, trans. *Doorkeeper of the Heart: versions of Rabi'a* . New York: Pir, 1988.

de Vitray-Meyerovitch, Eva. *Rumi and Sufism.* Sausalito, CA: Post-Apollo, 1987.

Wallis, Jim. *The Soul of Politics.* London: Fount, 1994.

Ward, Benedicta, trans. *The Sayings of the Desert Fathers.* Kalamazoo: Cistercian, 1984.

Ware, Kallistos. *The Inner Kingdom.* New York: St Vladimir's Seminary, 2000.

Webster, Jill Rosemary. *Els Menorets: The Franciscans in the Realms of Aragon from St. Francis to the Black Death.* Toronto: Pontifical Institute of Medieval Studies, 1993.

Welle, Jason. "Arabic Sources for the Encounter between the Saint and the Sultan: Fakhr al-Farisi's Famous Adventure with Francis, or Lack Thereof". *Studia Orientalia Christiana Collectanea 48–49* (2015–2016) . Musky, Cairo: Franciscan Centre of Christian Oriental Studies, 2019.

Wolpé, Sholeh. *The Conference of the Birds*. NY: W. W. Norton & Co, 2017.

Woodruff, Sue. *Meditations with Mechtild of Magdeburg*. Sante Fe, NM: Bear & Co., 1982.

Woods, Richard. *Mysticism and Prophecy: The Dominican Tradition*. London: Darton, Longman & Todd, 1998.